W9-AND-835

CALDWELL COLLEGE

JENNINGS LIBRARY

CALDWELL, NEW JERSEY 07006

JENNINGS LIBRARY

CALDWELL COLLEGE

King Arthur
and his Knights

Julek Heller and Deirdre Headon

DRAGON'S WORLD

398.220942
H43K

To

ANNE

[JH]

For my parents

P L H and M P H

with love and respect

[DH]

Dragon's World Ltd
Limpsfield
Surrey RH8 0DY
Great Britain

First published by Dragon's World Ltd 1990

© Dragon's World Ltd 1990
© Artwork Julek Heller 1990
© Text Deirdre Headon 1990

All rights reserved

Editor	Trish Burgess
Designer	John Leath, MSTD
Editorial Director	Pippa Rubinstein
Art Director	Dave Allen

No part of this book may be reproduced or transmitted in any form or by any means,
electronic or mechanical, including photocopy, recording, or any information storage
and retrieval system, without permission in writing from Dragon's World Limited,
except by a reviewer who may quote brief passages in a review.

British Library Cataloguing in Publication Data
Headon, Deirdre
    King Arthur and his Knights.
    I. Title   II. Malory, Thomas. Morte d'Arthur   III. Heller, Julek
823.2 [F]

ISBN 1 85028 114 9

Typeset by Flairplan Phototypesetting Ltd

Quality Printing and Binding by:
Khai Wah Litho Co Pte Ltd,
16 Kallang Place # 07-02
Singapore 1233
Republic of Singapore

161414

CONTENTS

The Coming of Arthur

The Knights of the Round Table

The Decline of Camelot

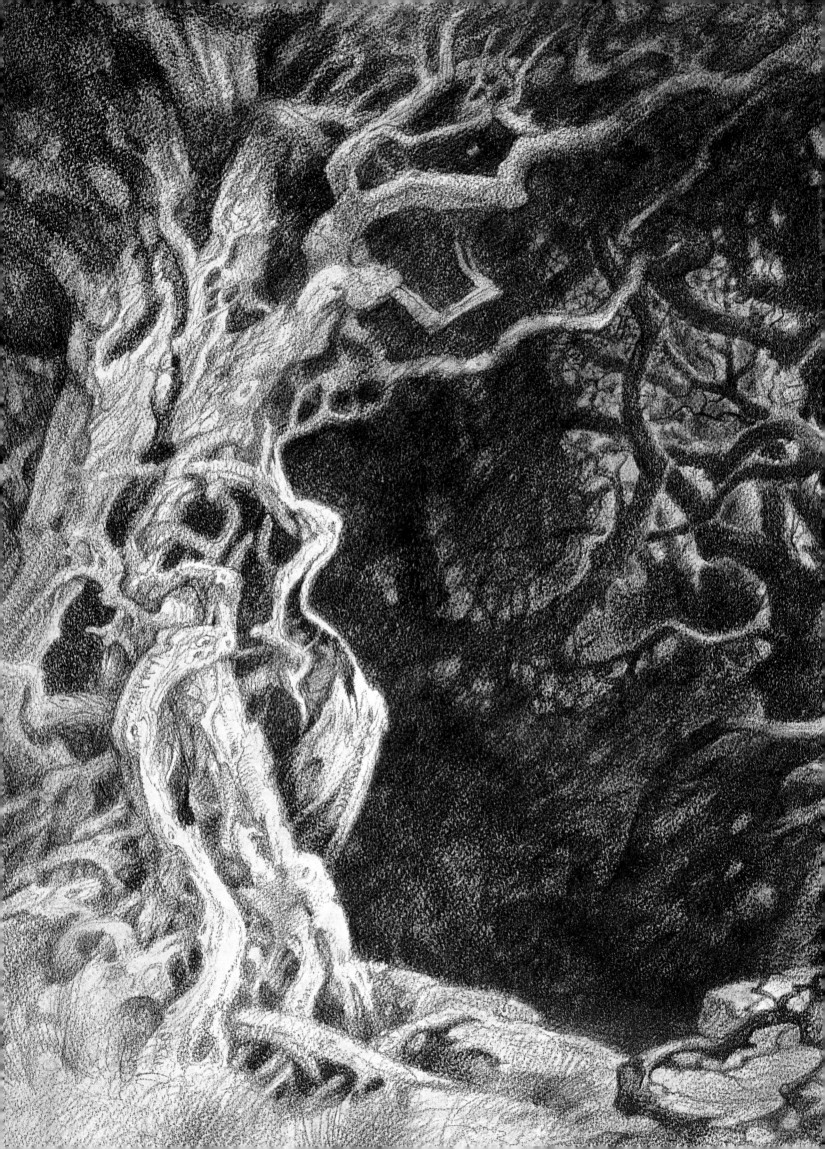

The Coming
of Arthur

Merlin

THIS IS THE NOBLE TALE of King Arthur, who first came to the land that is known as Britain many centuries ago, and whose lifetime saw many glorious events that are still spoken of even to this day.

At the time of Arthur, Britain was a land of magic and superstition where fairies, wizards and many other creatures lived in community with human beings. Yet it was also a dark and treacherous country, for its people had suffered through many war-torn years under the yoke of cruel, invading conquerors. When the Roman legions finally left these inhospitable shores to return to their homeland, Britain fell into brutal lawlessness and warring tribes savagely fought each other for supremacy. The country became a place of danger, where marauding tribesmen lurked in the forests, striking terror into all who met with them.

In time, Britain was invaded by Saxon warriors from the wild northern countries, who pillaged what poor settlements survived. Each morning, as the sun rose in the sky, the downtrodden Britons prayed to their gods that a great leader might be sent to unite them so that peace would once more be known in their land. But none came, and the years passed in bitter subjection to those conquering invaders who ruled by fear and the sword. None the less, throughout these difficult times, the people managed to survive by scratching a living from the reluctant soil.

Then came Vortigern - an evil man who sought to subjugate all who

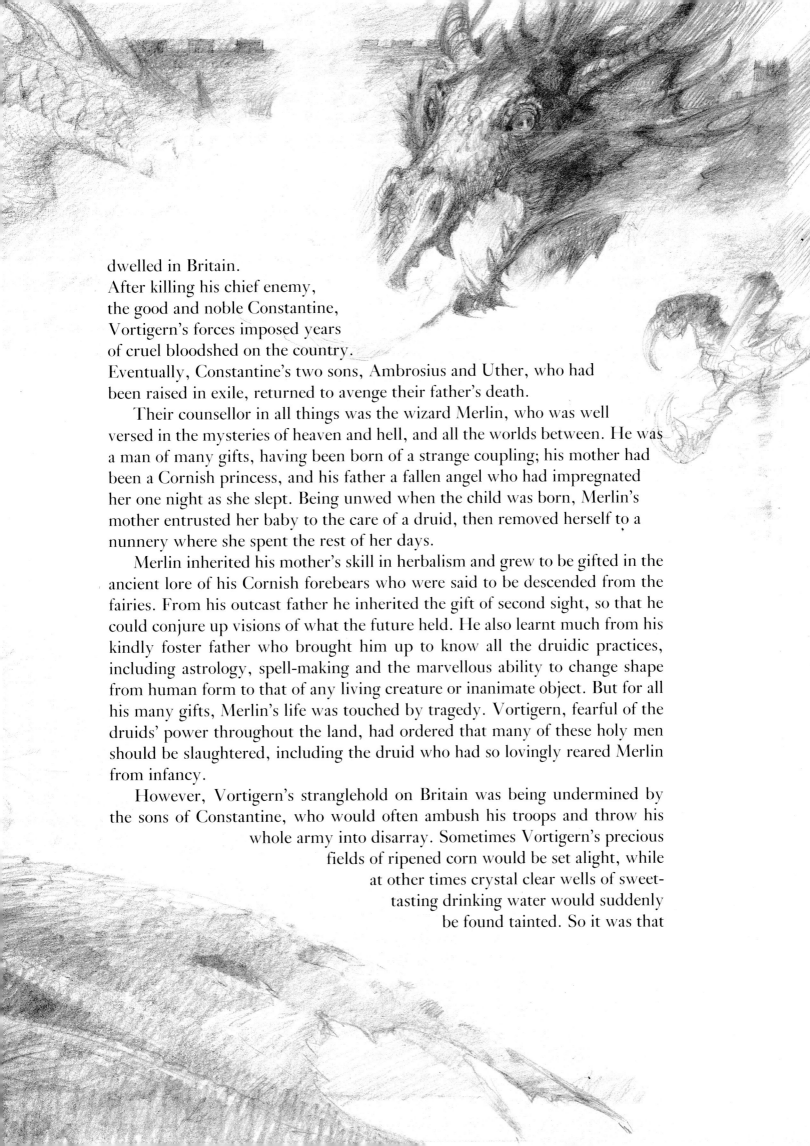

dwelled in Britain.
After killing his chief enemy,
the good and noble Constantine,
Vortigern's forces imposed years
of cruel bloodshed on the country.
Eventually, Constantine's two sons, Ambrosius and Uther, who had
been raised in exile, returned to avenge their father's death.

Their counsellor in all things was the wizard Merlin, who was well
versed in the mysteries of heaven and hell, and all the worlds between. He was
a man of many gifts, having been born of a strange coupling; his mother had
been a Cornish princess, and his father a fallen angel who had impregnated
her one night as she slept. Being unwed when the child was born, Merlin's
mother entrusted her baby to the care of a druid, then removed herself to a
nunnery where she spent the rest of her days.

Merlin inherited his mother's skill in herbalism and grew to be gifted in the
ancient lore of his Cornish forebears who were said to be descended from the
fairies. From his outcast father he inherited the gift of second sight, so that he
could conjure up visions of what the future held. He also learnt much from his
kindly foster father who brought him up to know all the druidic practices,
including astrology, spell-making and the marvellous ability to change shape
from human form to that of any living creature or inanimate object. But for all
his many gifts, Merlin's life was touched by tragedy. Vortigern, fearful of the
druids' power throughout the land, had ordered that many of these holy men
should be slaughtered, including the druid who had so lovingly reared Merlin
from infancy.

However, Vortigern's stranglehold on Britain was being undermined by
the sons of Constantine, who would often ambush his troops and throw his
whole army into disarray. Sometimes Vortigern's precious
fields of ripened corn would be set alight, while
at other times crystal clear wells of sweet-
tasting drinking water would suddenly
be found tainted. So it was that

Vortigern realized some great power was hungry for his destruction, and his foreboding was compounded when one day his soothsayer told him that ill fortune could only be kept at bay if he once more spilt druid blood in sacrifice to his gods.

So many druids had already been slaughtered that only a few remained at liberty. Merlin was such a man, and it was not long before someone betrayed his whereabouts for a small bag of silver. He was captured and brought in chains before Vortigern who wished to witness his execution.

'Are you not afraid that by sundown you will be dead?' demanded Vortigern, both irritated and bewildered by the young druid's nerveless composure. But Merlin, a knowing smile playing at the corners of his mouth, did not grace him with a reply. 'You die in a few hours, you stupid creature,' spluttered Vortigern in vexation. 'Do you value your life so little?'

With his power of foresight and ability to change shape in order to escape from danger, Merlin was quite untroubled by his apparent fate. 'If I am to be killed,' he said calmly, 'I ask you to grant me a boon before I die.' When Vortigern agreed, Merlin asked to be taken to a deep lake nearby. Intrigued by this request, Vortigern determined to accompany the druid. When they reached the lake, Merlin walked to the edge and stretched out his arms, drawing in a deep breath. As he exhaled, his breath flowed out over the lake, forming ripples which grew into foaming waves. These separated to expose two slumbering dragons on the lake's floor: one had white scaly skin while the other's was red, but none present knew what this omened

As if reading the onlookers' thoughts, Merlin explained. 'The red dragon symbolizes the Britons and the white the Saxons. While it is day, the creatures slumber as contentedly as two babies in the same cradle, but when night comes, they fight as if in mortal combat.'

'And what does this mean?' demanded Vortigern in a puzzled voice.

'It tells of the battle that is yet to come between you and the sons of Constantine,' answered Merlin.

'And who will win?' asked Vortigern, feeling a chill creep around his heart.

'The white dragon of the Saxons,' lied Merlin.

At the very moment he uttered these false words, he foresaw the mighty army of Ambrosius and Uther landing on the western coast of Britain and knew that they would soon be in this place as victors. Indeed, the following day the sons of Constantine joined battle against Vortigern and the mighty struggle began. Merlin fought as fiercely as the next man, but in the midst of the fighting he also watched over his brothers-in-arms, transporting

them through sorcery to another part of the battle when they met mortal danger.

To unbridled rejoicing throughout the land, cruel Vortigern was slain and Ambrosius, the elder son of Constantine, was crowned king. But before long, he too had died - poisoned by enemies, so it was rumoured. Thus, Uther, still mourning his brother's death, was proclaimed king.

Uther and Igraine

AFTER MANY A LONG YEAR, the hideous roar of war was at last gone from the land, and a fragile peace spread gently in its stead. Uther was crowned king and many believed his reign might herald a time of peace and prosperity. Merlin remained the king's chief adviser, keeping a watchful eye on the new monarch and often travelling with him through the kingdom. It was during such times that Merlin revealed to Uther tantalizing glimpses of his future. One midsummer's evening, as the two men walked along the beetling edge of a cliff in the lingering westerly light, they looked far out to sea and saw, clearly formed on the horizon, a billowing cloud in the shape of a dragon that burned fiery red against the fading light.

'What does this mean?' asked a puzzled Uther, for he knew that such a sign presaged some great omen.

'It is a sign of the greatness your son will possess,' answered Merlin. 'He will win glory far surpassing yours.' And it was in witness to this prophercy that Uther henceforth called himself Pendragon, meaning 'dragon's head'.

Uther longed for unity among the nobles in his kingdom, and it was to this end that he invited all the lords who were in some way opposed to his kingship to court. Some of his opponents believed this invitation to be a trap and feared that during the feasting, while lulled into a sense of security from good food and drink, they would be slaughtered by the king's soldiers, an occurrence often recounted in ancient tales.

However, evil of a different type was to be unleashed at court, and all because of the passions aroused by a woman's beauty. One of the king's most honoured guests was Gorlois, Duke of Cornwall, who had brought with him his beautiful wife Igraine. Her beauty was famed throughout the land, and though not yet thirty years of age, Igraine was the mother of three near-adult daughters. Her face was oval, like a droplet of dew fallen from a verdant leaf on a clear morning; her skin glowed with a peachy blush; and beneath her straight, dark brows gleamed eyes of the deepest blue. Her full mouth gave promise of a passionate nature, but this had not yet found expression, for her husband was some twenty years her senior and he had no inclination to be gentle with his fourteen-year-old bride whom he had wed to beget sons; although he loved his daughters well, they could not succeed to his dukedom.

Gorlois and Igraine had brought their two oldest daughters with them, for they were now of marriageable age and, they hoped, one might prove a suitable wife for King Uther as such an alliance would further cement peace between the new king and his recalcitrant nobles. However, the moment Uther's gaze fell upon Igraine he felt his heart flutter furiously in his breast and hot colour suffuse his face. Raised only to desire vengeance, he was bemused by these first stirrings of love, and succumbed entirely to this benevolent disease.

The king had planned to lavish gifts upon his guests, but now the only gifts he sent were to the Duke of Cornwall's quarters: breathtaking bracelets wrought from Welsh gold and studded with jewels, together with fabulously designed garments laced with golden threads.

Igraine had immediately sensed how greatly Uther desired her and she grew increasingly concerned as he continued to court her for she knew her husband to be a jealous man. At first she persuaded Gorlois that these daily gifts were but tokens sent to their daughters, but eventually the duke could not mistake the king's admiration for his wife. When dancing, Uther's eyes lingered longingly on Igraine's graceful form and his arms frequently clasped her longer than the dance demanded.

Gorlois stormed from the great hall in a frenzy of jealousy, dragging a terrified Igraine in his train. 'I have been betrayed. I have been made a cuckold,' he ranted and railed against his stainless wife when they had once more reached their quarters. 'Any child you bear now I will not acknowledge as my blood.' Igraine could do or say nothing to lessen her husband's feeling of betrayal, and that night, at his urgent behest, the whole entourage left Uther's castle, galloping furiously to put a night's ride between the king and the Duke of Cornwall's family.

Gorlois knew that this action might provoke war, but so strongly did he feel that Uther had sullied his reputation, that he was prepared to take the risk. Taking his wife and daughters to the safety of Tintagel Castle, he then mustered such forces as he could and quickly made his way to Castle Terrabil and prepared for the siege that Uther was certain to lay against them.

The prospect of another war so soon after peace had been established

appalled Uther's counsellors, so they persuaded the king to start by issuing an ultimatum to the duke: if the duke did not return to court with his wife within fourteen days, King Uther would have no option but to declare war. When this message reached Castle Terrabil, the duke fell into an even greater rage and, careless of any danger to himself, rode unaccompanied to Tintagel to tell Igraine what turn events had taken. While there, Gorlois also made certain that his three daughters knew his version of King Uther's treachery.

'If I should die in the battle that will soon come, I charge you, my well-beloved daughters, to avenge my death.' So saying, he solemnly drew out his sword so that his daughters, Elaine, Margawse and Morgan, might swear on it. Without hesitation, all did so, and Morgan le Fay, the youngest and most ardent of the sisters, made another vow that she held close in her heart – that if her father should die at the hands of Uther or his army, then she would take revenge on all of Uther's blood.

Igraine, who was a good and gentle woman, rued the day that she had been born with so much beauty. As she sat huddled in warm furs against the damp coldness of her private chamber, she gazed into the flickering flames of the fire that burned in the hearth and recalled the prophecy of an old woman who had once sought shelter at her father's castle. When this woman had first looked upon the child Igraine she had recoiled as if privy to some dread secret. Then she had foretold how Igraine would grow most fair and bring death to all men who loved her. Now her prophecy seemed about to be fulfilled. Igraine wished with all her heart that she had chosen a life of seclusion rather than bring sorrow to the world where men might see and love her.

Winter, with its chill breath, had frozen the bleak land and even the birds had ceased to chirrup and sing. All this while Uther's army was encamped, frozen like blocks of ice on the exposed and wind-chilled land that lay around Castle Terrabil. Despite the inhospitable conditions and grim fortifications that confronted them, Uther refused to lift the siege. Fierce skirmishes saw many good soldiers lost on both sides, but little progress was made in the conflict as both sides were evenly matched in strength and fighting prowess. As the days passed with numbing monotony, a lacklustre Uther fell sick, his desire for Igraine abating not a jot but gnawing inside him like an insatiable hunger.

'Merlin, where are you when I have most need of you?' cried Uther into the dark night air one chill evening. 'Answer me, I beg you, Merlin.' So it was that Merlin, deep within his underground refuge in the forest, heard Uther's supplication. And when he first saw Uther, he discerned at once the cause of his sickness, knowing that the events he had seen in Uther's future were shortly to come about.

'If it is really your heart's desire, then Igraine can be yours,' said Merlin, knowing that such words would only tantalize Uther further. 'But there will be a high price to pay for satisfying your desire.'

'I will do anything,' said Uther with a deep sigh, 'even if it be to forfeit my kingdom, for I must have her.' At this Merlin's face grew sad as he knew the king had promised something he would come to regret.

'Then you shall lie with Igraine tonight,' said Merlin gravely. 'I prophesize that a male child will be conceived but he is to be given into my care an hour from his birth. I shall protect your child and see that he is reared in safety, for turbulent times will come again to this kingdom. Do you swear to this?' Uther nodded in agreement.

That night Merlin drew on all his powers of enchantment, bringing from deep within himself the awesome power of the dragon. Chanting a secret charm, he wove around Uther a magic mist so that the king's shape changed and he took on the appearance of the Duke of Cornwall. With Merlin as his guide, Uther mounted his horse and galloped towards Tintagel where Igraine lay. On arriving, he readily gained admittance as the guards believed him to be their duke. As Uther climbed the stone steps that led to Igraine's chamber, only the duke's favourite hound knew that this man was not his master. But Merlin quieted the dog by blowing the dragon's breath over its growling form and it fell down in a deep sleep.

Igraine welcomed Uther as if he were Gorlois, and meekly followed him when he insisted that they retire to her bedchamber. As Merlin had foretold, that night, high above the foaming sea at Tintagel, Arthur of Britain was conceived. In later years, many people spoke in wonder of that night, for on the bleak castle's battlements a missel-thrush, harbinger of momentous events, had been heard singing all through the hours of darkness.

At daybreak Merlin came into the bedchamber, breathing in its honeyed warmth as he gazed upon the couple sleeping peacefully entwined in each other's arms.

'We must flee this castle before the enchantment fades,' whispered Merlin in Uther's ear. The king rose at once and the two men made their way quickly out of the castle, passing safely by the still dozing guards.

'I must wed her,' groaned Uther, as they rode away. 'I love her beyond my very life.'

'Be patient, Uther,' counselled Merlin. 'You will marry Igraine in time.'

Unbeknown to Uther, just as he had entered the gates of Tintagel the night before, the Duke of Cornwall had been slain in a raid he had launched against Uther's camp. When news of the duke's death was brought to her the next day, Igraine's heart was full of sorrow. But as she heard the details, it became clear that he had died before his apparent visit to her. Who, then, was the man who had lain with her last night? Fear and grief weighed upon her, but she knew she must keep this perturbing secret to herself.

After an appropriate period of mourning had passed, Uther visited Tintagel and began to court Igraine. When he asked her to become his wife, she revealed what had happened on the night her husband died, confessing that now she was with child but did not know who had fathered it. Uther loved her all the more for her honesty and he told her of Merlin's magic and of what he had prophesized for their child. So it was with an easy heart that Igraine agreed to become Uther's wife.

The months passed quickly and the queen grew large with child. Merlin, who had been absent from court, now reappeared as the birth drew near.

'Do you remember what you promised me, Uther?' asked Merlin.

At first Uther feigned ignorance, but then he reluctantly acknowledged their bargain, saying, 'But I do not like it, nor does the queen.'

'You will have other children,' said Merlin. 'All I ask is that you keep the promise you made to me.'

'So be it,' said Uther at last, for he knew he could not escape his bargain with the wizard, and it was quite possible that his nobles might not accept this child as his true heir. Merlin then told Uther of his plans for the infant: he

would be placed in the household of one Sir Ector whose wife had but a few months earlier given birth to a son.

'Let me send for Sir Ector,' continued Merlin, 'so you may see that he is most fit to be foster father to your child.'

When Uther saw this knight, he recognized him as a loyal man who would treat his child with respect.

Close by the feast of Christmas the queen was delivered of her child. Although the thought of separation gave Igraine and Uther much pain, they parted with their child. Each gave the infant their blessing. Uther wrapped his unnamed son in a sumptuous cloth of gold and took the tiny babe down to a small gateway that led out of the castle. Here, an old man with a grey beard and shrouded in a voluminous black cloak took the baby and disappeared into the darkness.

Morgan, the queen's youngest child, had stayed close by her mother all through her confinement and when she saw her stepfather take the baby from her piteously weeping mother, she followed to see what he did with it. Thus, Morgan was the only witness of these events and the only other person who knew that the king was lying when he announced to the court that the new-born prince had died.

Although tender in years, Morgan was blessed (some would say cursed) with fairy blood that had been strong in her parents' forebears. As yet, this little creature knew nothing of her powers of enchantment; all she understood was that her father had gone from her and the man who replaced him filled her with dread.

Two days' journey from Tintagel, Merlin reached the castle of Sir Ector. This good knight's wife immediately took pity on the squealing bundle and clasped

him to her breast, from which she had recently weaned her own son Kay. At once the tiny babe sucked ravenously and Merlin smiled, knowing that the precious child would thrive in this household. Before leaving, the wizard called for a priest to christen the infant and he was named Arthur.

The Sword in the Stone

ARTHUR GREW BY LEAPS AND BOUNDS, safe in Sir Ector's bustling household, where he was always treated as a member of the family. He grew into a fine, strong boy who never knew a day's sickness and by the time he was eight years old he could run like the wind and swim like a fish. He was already a fine horseman who could spring unaided into the saddle, and he had also learnt to wield a sword and to use a lance by tilting at the quintain.

A good-natured boy, always willing to run errands, Arthur bore with good grace the bullying of his foster brother Kay who believed him to be the base-born son of some great knight and therefore deserving of such treatment. When, at fourteen, Kay became a squire, Arthur served as his page and attended him in all things. Arthur longed for the day when he too would be a knight but he held little hope of this happening for he could not prove his knightly pedigree. At such moments of yearning, he wondered who his parents really were.

All this time Merlin kept watch over Arthur, shifting his shape into that of many creatures to safeguard the future king from any danger. Sometimes Merlin was a soaring bird in the sky or a bee that buzzed busily around Arthur as he rushed through the sun-dappled woods and summer fields on some boyish escapade. In winter he would shift into the guise of a tree, watching Arthur with eyes disguised as woody knots in the bark. His favourite shape, however, was that of a dragonfly, which dipped and dived in the air as it followed Arthur at play. At the right time Merlin planned to make himself known to the boy and reveal his great destiny.

Favourite of all Kay's and Arthur's activities was hawking. To see the bird soaring high in the sky, then diving at speed to snatch its trembling prey from the ground below, made their young yet cruel hearts beat faster. Arthur often tended the birds in the mews where they were housed and was sometimes allowed to take them out under the watchful supervision of Sir Ector. However, it was expressly forbidden for either Kay or Arthur to hold the birds unless they were accompanied by an adult, for they were exceedingly valuable and could not be easily controlled once off the hand.

One fine clear summer's morning Kay and Arthur awoke and immediately fell to arguing as they jumped up from the straw pallets on which they slept in

the great hall. As was often
the case, their dispute concerned hawking and Kay
argued that Arthur would never be
worthy to handle Sir Ector's hawk.

'Only a trueborn man can handle
a hawk,' claimed Kay.

'I am as trueborn as you,' replied Arthur hotly.

'You are not,' retorted Kay.

'I am in truth,' said Arthur. 'And I will prove
it.' Refusing to tolerate this
slur on his character, he stormed down to the mews,
waited until the keeper was distracted and then, putting
a leather gauntlet on his right hand, he took Sir Ector's
favourite falcon, its little head covered with a leather hood, down
from its perch. The movement made the tiny silver bell
attached to its claw by a leather jesse start to tinkle.

Arthur scampered quickly away from the mews until
he reached the meadows that lay below the castle. Here, he
started to imitate how he had seen Sir Ector fly his falcon - removing the hood and throwing the bird off his wrist. The noble bird
immediately flew high into the clear blue sky, diving, soaring
and revelling in her new-found freedom. Spying a plump
rat, she swooped down to snatch her prey, but nothing
Arthur did would lure her back on to his wrist. Now
distraught with fear, for Sir Ector would surely
punish him severely for taking his favourite falcon,
Arthur decided to make one last effort
to catch the bird.

The hawk had come to rest on the branch of a tree at the edge of the forest, but as Arthur approached she flew haphazardly ahead of him. He continued in dogged pursuit for some time, but then he noticed that the sun, which had earlier spread its dappled light through the trees, had now all but disappeared. Soon it would be night.

Arthur was becoming increasingly frightened and wished that, whatever the consequences, he was back at the castle. As if to make matters worse, he began to think of all the wild beasts that came out in the dark. Both he and Kay were wont to terrify each other at night with gruesome tales of creatures which dwelled in the forest near the castle – the wolfman who ate children, and the two-headed carrion crow who sucked blood. Arthur started to cry, and as he sobbed he said out loud, in a tiny, quavering voice, a rhyme which helped when either he or Kay had bad dreams.

> Sleep tight, spirits of night,
> Beasts that bite, fleas that fight
> To suck my blood. Begone! Begone!

However, Merlin had been following Arthur's steps closely, turning to stone any creature who ventured too near the boy. Protected by this unseen power, Arthur wandered deeper into the forest and when it had become completely dark, the lonely, hungry and begrimed little boy found a pile of dry leaves, buried himself among them for warmth and promptly fell asleep. All night long Merlin stood guard over the sleeping boy. When the dawn came, Merlin left and went to his dwelling nearby, for Arthur would meet him later that day.

As the sun warmed Arthur's face with its first light, he stirred and stretched. He had rested so well that at first he did not remember where he was. Then, when he recalled, he wished he had remained asleep; he was still hungry, still lost and still searching for Sir Ector's falcon. He sat up and stayed quite still, listening to the sounds of the forest. The branches of the great trees swayed to and fro in the gentle breeze that seemed to whisper through the forest. The very air seemed full of noise. Even the sun, as it danced on the trees, undergrowth and ground, was alive and full of movement and colour. Arthur no longer felt afraid; he was captivated by the calling of animals whose names he did not know and the birds he had never seen before who filled the forest with their song.

Arthur knew that the sound and direction of distant hoofbeats could be heard by putting an ear to the ground; perhaps he could use the same technique to discover if a search party were coming to look for him. Placing his ear to the

ground, the only sound he could distinguish was that of water trickling nearby. He struck out in that direction, thinking that he could at least find some water to drink, and soon came to a clearing in the forest where he saw a tumbledown cottage. Someone obviously lived there, for a thin wisp of smoke was puffing from the chimney up through the trees and high into the sky. As he looked around, Arthur saw a very strange old man with a long, grey beard and long, grey hair bending over the stream that ran close by and picking watercress that glistened dark and green. Brushing himself down, for he knew that his night in the forest had left him somewhat dishevelled, Arthur walked over to the old man, who seemed to sense his approach, as he turned and lifted his head to greet him.

'Would you like some of this to eat?' asked Merlin, for that is who the old man was.

'Thank you, sir,' said Arthur, who longed for something more substantial to eat. 'But if I could have anything at all to eat, it would be a trencher of bread and some meat.'

'Really?' said Merlin. He smiled to himself, then covered the watercress in one hand, made a swirling motion with the other, then opened his hand to

reveal some newly-baked, soft, white bread and a succulent serving of venison. Arthur's mouth immediately began to water as he savoured the aroma of the roast meat.

'Eat well, and then we will get better acquainted,' said Merlin, gesturing Arthur to sit on the ground as he ate.

'Thank you so much,' mumbled Arthur gratefully, his mouth bulging with food. In a very short time the food was gone.

'Now I expect you want a drink,' said Merlin. He filled his cupped hands with water from the stream, blew on it and it was immediately transformed into a beaker of foaming, warm milk. Although Arthur did not like milk greatly, when this drink passed his lips it tasted like nectar. Revived by the food, he now looked at the old man as if for the first time and saw that he had a kind and gentle face. When he looked on his countenance Arthur felt secure and safe from harm.

'Thank you so much for this food,' said Arthur. 'It was most generous of you to feed me.' Sir Ector had always been rigorous that his boys should show good manners and respect to their elders.

'The stars have long foretold that I should help you,' said Merlin, somewhat to Arthur's bewilderment. 'Come, let us go into my house and I will tell you how I know about you.'

Inside the cottage Arthur found the most intriguing room he had ever seen, piled high with many strange objects. So unlike the sparsely furnished castle where he lived, here there was not a bit of space that was not cluttered with strange bottles filled with many coloured liquids. The room was scented with a cloying sweetness and Arthur thought the smell seemed to be coming from the dried herbs and roots that were hanging in numerous tied bundles from the ceiling. In one place he thought he saw the skull of a sheep, and elsewhere a human skull. And there were books and more books stacked high around the room and all these teetering piles seemed to be covered in dust, as if none had been opened for a very long time. While Arthur was taking in his surroundings, Merlin sat down at a dusty table on which there were more books.

'Do you want to see your future?' asked Merlin without further ado.

'How is that possible?' asked Arthur in a puzzled voice. 'Surely no one can do that.'

'Watch me,' said Merlin. The wizard then pored over a great volume whose open pages were filled with many strange symbols but no words that Arthur could see. He seemed to have completely forgotten that Arthur was in the

room as his finger marked a spot on an open page and he began to mumble incomprehensible words under his breath. Next he stood up and from deep within his chest there was began to issue a deep groan, and as the groan rose in his throat, blue smoke poured slowly from his mouth, filling the room and obscuring everything. The smoke seemed to concentrate in front of Arthur, who sat down on the floor in amazement at what was happening. Gradually, the smoky cloud began to take shape and in it Arthur could see the outline, albeit a little indistinct, of a great castle built high on a hill above a thick forest. Along a steep path leading up to the castle he saw many knights cantering in line. On the castle battlements fluttered a flag blazoned with the fiery sign of the dragon. Arthur was greatly intrigued and wondered what it all meant.

'This is your destiny, Arthur,' said Merlin in a solemn tone. 'Remember the dragon and this shall always guide you.' The smoke melted away and Arthur rubbed his eyes, uncertain of what he had seen. If he had been dreaming, then it was a wonderful dream which he must remember so that he could tell Kay.

'You must go now Arthur,' Merlin whispered huskily, seeming suddenly exhausted as he ushered the boy out of the house. Once outside, Arthur saw the missing falcon resting on the branch of a nearby tree. As he approached it, the bird immediately took flight, but the jingling of the silver bell on her claw guided Arthur safely out of the forest and back to the castle.

Although pleased at his return, nobody believed his strange adventure. All were convinced that he had eaten some root which had given him peculiar imaginings - something that often happened to hermits who lived in forests. Arthur was greatly surprised not to be beaten for his escapade, but Sir Ector and his weeping wife were too relieved and happy to have their foster son back unharmed to think of punishing him. Arthur was whisked off to Sir Ector's own feather bed with a bowl of soft, white bread soaked in warm milk and sweetened with honey where he slept for twenty-four hours and awoke wondering if his adventure had been nothing more than a dream.

Many years passed and Arthur grew into a fine youth, each year bringing him closer to the time when he would fulfil his destiny. It was Christmas once again and, as was the custom at this time, many knights were gathered in Winchester for a great tournament that followed the feast days. Sir Ector's son Kay, who had been recently knighted, was eager to take part in his first tournament, and Arthur, filled with excitement, was to accompany him as his squire.

It was a merry band that set out for Winchester from Sir Ector's castle, singing loudly as they left on a cold December morning, their warm breath billowing around them in swirling clouds as it met the frosty morning air. But the weather proved so harsh that the journey took two days longer than anticipated and they only arrived in Winchester on the morning of the tourney itself with barely enough time for Kay and Sir Ector to arm themselves and ride into the lists. Kay, not unnaturally, was feeling anxious about his first tourney, and Arthur's clumsiness in dressing and arming him did not ease the situation. He kept misplacing important items of dress, provoking Kay's vicious temper. At last it appeared that everything was ready and Kay went to mount his powerful destrier. Arthur stood at his side carrying all the lances that Kay might require, as well as his axe and mace.

'Where is my sword?' shouted Kay, as he made to ride off. 'How do you think I can fight without one?'

'I must have left it at the lodgings,' said Arthur with a wail, quickly moving out of reach of Kay's bad-tempered kick. Dropping all the weaponry he was carrying, Arthur sped back to the lodgings to search for the sword which had been specially commissioned by Sir Ector for Kay and which was to have been

the only sword he would possess during his life as a knight. On their journey Kay had told his companions how he had named his sword 'Courageous', for it would make him so in every combat as it was such a fine weapon. Now, Arthur could find no sign of the sword and was greatly distressed. Kay will never forgive me for losing it, he thought.

Then he remembered a strange sight he had seen in a churchyard as he had run by. He raced back to that spot and there, standing straight and bright in the midst of mossy and weatherbeaten tombstones, was a fine sword. But when he went close up to it he saw that the blade was firmly embedded in a large stone. Arthur decided to borrow the sword, so he stood over it, clasped both hands tightly around the hilt and pulled with all his might. Nothing happened. Raising his eyes to heaven and muttering a prayer under his breath, he tried again. This time it seemed as if the watery winter sun suddenly blazed on him with midsummer heat, and this time the sword slid easily from the stone as simply as if he were drawing it from a scabbard. The air around him seemed to hum some mysterious angelic melody, but Arthur had no time to lose. He held the sword close to his chest and ran, fleet-footed as a deer, from the churchyard to where Sir Ector and Sir Kay were waiting with mounting impatience. The tournament was about to begin.

'But this is not my sword,' moaned Kay when Arthur gave him the sword he had taken from the graveyard.

'"Courageous" has been stolen,' said Arthur in a quiet voice.

'What!' exploded Sir Ector incredulously. 'That sword is irreplaceable. Do you know what care I took to get that sword?' And he boxed Arthur's ears.

However, Arthur won a small respite from their anger for the two knights could not delay to beat him or they would miss the mêlée. Chastened, he followed them to the lists, where he crept to the sidelines and watched open-mouthed at the colourful spectacle just unfolding. The field was alive with many different pennants, each one being a knight's personal standard, as well as that of the team on whose side he fought.

At last, the mêlée began. The teams of knights rode towards each other at full tilt. Soon the tournament ground resounded with the clash of weapons on armour, as well as warlike cries and cursing when a knight was knocked from his horse. Arthur watched the whole spectacle as if mesmerized and longed for the day when he might participate in such a glorious event.

Meanwhile, an old priest who had been at prayer in the churchyard and witnessed Arthur pulling the sword from the stone had rushed to the tournament ground to tell of this great event.

'We have a king!' he shouted, rushing into the lists and waving his arms in excitement. The knights paid him scant attention, but so great was his fervour to impart this great news that he rushed into the thick of the fighting. 'I have seen the man who is to be our king,' bellowed the priest. 'I have seen him draw the sword from the stone.' When this cry was heard, it stopped the tournament, for every man knew the prophecy attached to the sword. It had been foretold that whosoever drew the sword from the stone would be the rightful king of all Britain. Indeed, there was not a knight in the land who had not tried to draw out the sword.

'Well, where is our king?' shouted a knight.

'Yes, where is he?' clamoured another. 'How can we believe you when we have not seen it with our own eyes?'

Soon all the knights took up this doubting cry and the priest was roused to anger. Standing his ground, he asked each knight to look at his sword, for surely one of them would possess the sword from the stone. Thus it was to Kay's complete astonishment that he was found to have the sword.

'Then I must be king,' proclaimed Kay, albeit a little uncertainly.

'Are you certain that this can be so?' asked his father. At this point, as he stood under the close scrutiny of the most fearsome knights in the land, Kay's courage failed him.

'No father,' he admitted. 'Arthur gave me this sword.'

'Arthur?' said Sir Ector incredulously. At this, all the knights demanded that Arthur step forward so they might see him.

'Where is Arthur?' they cried, as of a single voice.

'This Arthur must be our king,' cried certain knights.

'Let us see him and hear what he has to say,' said others.

And as their voices rose in a clamour, a single word was heard uttered clearly above the din; and this word was the name Arthur.

When the boy came forward everybody laughed out loud, for this simple-looking squire could surely not be their king. They had not waited through so many difficult, leaderless years for a beardless, callow youth. Arthur was greatly angered that they should joke at him, so with unmistakable authority, which made Sir Ector and Kay stare in wonder, he faced them all and made a declaration.

'If you desire it, I will show you how I drew the sword from the stone, sir knights,' said Arthur with an imperious air.

All those present at the tournament made their way to the churchyard and, once assembled, Arthur put the sword back into the stone.

'Any man who wishes may try to draw the sword out again,' said Arthur, pointing proudly towards the blade he had replaced. Both Sir Ector and Kay tried in vain, as did many other knights who had come to see this wonder. Finally, Arthur came forward once more and, holding the sword's hilt in his right hand, he drew the blade out with graceful ease. All those gathered fell as silent as the tombs themselves, not knowing what to make of what they had seen. However, at this very moment Merlin appeared in the churchyard, looking for all the world as if he had risen out of one of the tombs itself. Glancing this way and that, he made his way forward to where Arthur stood.

'Why, it is you, my old friend from the forest,' said Arthur in wonder.

'It is I,' said Merlin. Now many of the older knights remembered Merlin from when Uther ruled the land, and they also remembered how much the king had heeded this druid's counsel. Without further ado, Merlin told the expectant crowd the true story of Arthur's birth.

'Why yes,' said Sir Ector, 'I recall that gold cloak. If I remember right it is still in the chest at my castle.' Suddenly, the great import of these events dawned on him and, pulling Kay down with him, he knelt in homage to their new king. A bright tear glistened on this good knight's weatherbeaten cheek as he thought of the trust that had been placed in him by his old comrade-in-arms, King Uther, whom he had loved and served well.

Arthur was both bemused and embarrassed by their actions, and even more so when the old priest came forward to crown him with a circlet of gold which had been in the safe-keeping of this very church for the time when the new king should come to claim it.

'God protect the king,' cried the gathered crowd, as they carried Arthur high on their shoulders to the castle in the town that is now called Winchester.

There was unrestrained rejoicing that Britain once more had a king to rule over the land, and the people took great delight that their new king was so fresh and young a man, filled with vitality for whatever great adventures lay ahead. The story of how he had been made king travelled through the country like wildfire, and many a fair maid's head was turned with thoughts of this delightful young king who was not yet married.

The first challenge to Arthur's monarchy came from the north of his kingdom, where forces were being mustered by rebellious lords, the chief of them being King Lot of Orkney and the King of Scotland. In fact, many of these rebels travelled to Caerleon in Wales where Arthur was to be crowned with all the pomp and ceremony due to his high state. However, they all refused to attend the coronation or to swear allegiance to King Arthur, even when the young king sent them gifts and attempted to win their support in a variety of ways. If the truth be known, these lords sought war against a High King they judged to

be weak and lacking in the necessary power to be overlord throughout the land. They attacked Arthur as he came from the great church where he had been newly annointed and crowned, and so great was their number that he and his followers were forced to barricade themselves in a tower close by. At once, the northern lords lay siege to it, but after some days, Arthur, displaying his father's great courage, rode out alone to sue for peace and this brave stand won him many new supporters.

Nevertheless, this courageous gesture did not appease the northern lords and, before many days had passed, the rebels attacked the tower in which Arthur remained besieged. Soon, it looked as if the walls of this stronghold would be breached, but then the townsfolk of Caerleon, armed only with clubs and staves, came to fight valorously for their new king. Victory was nearly theirs, but Merlin told Arthur that he was not destined to rout their forces completely that day. The young king heeded Merlin's counsel, and thus allowed the northern lords to retreat.

King Arthur and his court rode to London and when it was midsummer, Merlin came again to Arthur and told him that he would soon face another challenge from the lords of the north. This time, however, their forces would be swelled by many mercenaries, and Merlin advised that Arthur should not engage in battle until he too had increased the fighting strength of his army.

And so it was that Arthur sailed across the sea to France where he hoped his envoys could persuade the good and powerful brothers, King Ban and King Bors, to join forces with him. Having survived many perils to reach their destination, the envoys soon obtained the brothers' pledge to fight for King Arthur, and a promise that they would arrive in England to fight for his cause by All-Hallows Day. In return, Arthur pledged that he would do the brothers a similar service when they should ask it of him.

Without delay, Arthur returned to London, where he decreed that a great tournament should be held immediately after the arrival of the brave French knights so that they might practise their world-renowned skills against his mettlesome English knights for the war that would soon follow. Every knight who took part in this glorious event conducted himself with all the courage and chivalry that such an occasion demanded. Watching from a flag-festooned dais, the ladies of the court participated in the tourney too, flirting gracefully with the French knights who all responded in kind with delightful courtesy.

Meanwhile, Arthur and his pre-eminent warriors discussed the strategy for the coming battle. Still lacking the necessary forces to be victorious, it was agreed that Merlin should try to recruit more in France, while two knights, Sir Grastian and Sir Placidas, should govern Ban's and Bors' lands in their absence.

Merlin chose only those knights whose fighting skills were best suited for warfare in Britain and these hand-picked warriors were shipped, in secret, to Dover. Of the 10,000 horsemen who rallied to Arthur's cause, only 5000 were equipped to fight in Britain.

Meanwhile, the northern lords were planning their revenge, having raised a fearsome force of over 70,000 mounted warriors, which vastly outnumbered even King Arthur's newly mustered army. The battle that was soon to be engaged would without doubt determine whose rule would hold sway throughout the land.

Merlin counselled that if the king's forces attacked by night, then what they lacked in fighting numbers they would gain through the advantage of surprise. On the appointed night thousands of horsemen moved silently towards the northern forces; the horses' hooves were muffled with cloth, all the jangling harnesses were removed and cloaks were thrown over armour to muffle any sounds that might betray movement.

Despite these precautions, somehow the enemy's sentries were disturbed and the northern lords responded swiftly and fiercely to this unexpected night attack. Many brave men were killed, but it was only in the first watery light of dawn that the carnage of the previous night was fully revealed. All through the

next day the battled raged, and when each force looked upon those who had been slain, they turned upon their enemy with renewed vigour.

Fortunately, before the battle had commenced, Merlin had hidden 10,000 fresh men, commanded by Ban and Bors, in nearby woodland. Here, they were instructed to remain hidden from sight until the agreed sign was given. But two over-zealous knights, Sir Lyonese and Sir Phariance, hearing the din of battle, could no longer restrain their desire to join the fray. Thinking they saw the enemy leaders tiring, they rushed their troops forward without authority. What they had, in fact, witnessed was the northern leaders temporarily withdrawing from the battle to rest, leaving the exhausted King Idres in command of the field.

From the vantage of their resting place, the rebel leaders thought their eyes deceived them when they spotted the standards of Bor and Ban being carried into the field. They had no idea that the French kings were even in the country. Without delay they remounted their horses and rejoined the battle.

Before long, only half of Arthur's 30,000 warriors remained alive. Merlin counselled the king to retreat as he could not win the day, so Arthur's army scattered rapidly throughout the countryside. His last order before this retreat was that any spoils from the battlefield should be given to Ban and Bors so that they might reward their brave knights. Through this gesture Arthur hoped that these fine warriors might fight for him again one day.

Arthur's valiant conduct in this battle caused many lesser kings, lords and knights to swear allegiance to him. However, his youthful exuberance had been tempered by war and he was now possessed of a wisdom that belied his youth.

As the months passed, more nobles defected from the rebellious cause of the northern lords as they saw how Arthur's rule stood for a time of peace and prosperity. After several years had passed, all the northern lands were subdued, and the time drew near when the noble order of the Round Table would be established.

Morgan le Fay

RUMOUR GALLOPED THROUGH THE LAND like a careering horse, bringing the portentous news that a mere slip of a lad would be king. When report of this reached Morgan le Fay, she sent messengers to her sisters, Margawse now

wedded to King Lot of Orkney, and Elaine who was queen of the Outer Isles, bidding them hasten to meet her at Tintagel Castle. Some weeks later they gathered in their dead father's castle to plot treason against their half-brother, though no women could have looked less like evil plotters. The three sisters shone with a beauty far beyond compare - all had glorious, flame-coloured hair, their faces were dominated by limpid green eyes and their unblemished skin looked as pale and smooth as alabaster. How could these vengeful women possibly be the offspring of the good and gentle Igraine? It was the blood of the irascible Duke of Cornwall that ran strong in their veins, and despite their frail bodies, they possessed the stout hearts of warriors, never shrinking from whatever dark deeds were demanded of them to accomplish their deepest desires. As huntresses rather than the hunted, the sisters sought the death of Arthur, for they had sworn to avenge their father's death on all of Uther's bloodline - and Morgan le Fay was to be the instrument through which this was to come about.

She was the fairest of the three sisters, standing straight and strong with long, gently curling hair, as flaming red as the fiery setting sun. Her face was cunning and her feline eyes changed colour as the daylight changed - from watery green in the brightest morning to the hard, glinting emerald of night. Her skin, as pale as death, sometimes made her resemble a carved marble statue of the Roman goddess Venus whose image could still be found throughout the land. However, in temper she resembled nothing more than the huntress Diana.

Morgan le Fay was well versed in the magic arts, for she had made a study of ancient scripts containing arcane spells. When Uther had married her mother, he soon found the surly presence of his beloved wife's youngest daughter more than he could bear, so he had her sent to a nunnery far away from court. It was here that Morgan le Fay became adept at changing her shape, concocting strange spells, summoning up fiendish creatures and, above all, looking through the mists of time to see far into the future and long into the past. These skills, combined with her Cornish fairy blood, meant that she had much in common with the powerful magic of Merlin.

When King Bors and King Ban left Britain for France after their support of King Arthur, Morgan le Fay went to Camelot, the seat of Arthur's court, to discover how she might bring about his destruction. She arrived in disguise, revealing her identity to no one. As she glided into the great hall, garbed in a robe of intricate design that glittered with jewels, she was a breathtaking figure, gleaming as bright as the Northern Lights.

Weary of war, and desirous of some gentle diversion, Arthur was entranced by this vision of loveliness, and from the very moment she arrived, he courted her persistently. Morgan le Fay caught her breath when she gazed upon the young king, for the looks of Uther were stamped so plainly on his face that all her stored-up hatred began to flow through her veins like a deadly poison. At Arthur's express instructions, she sat next to him at dinner the night after her arrival. Noticing that she ate only the daintiest pickings, Arthur shared the choicest morsels from his plate with her and then entreated her to visit him in his private apartments.

Later, Morgan le Fay waited in anticipation in her chamber. Her glorious hair fell in rippling waves to her knees. Eventually, a sleepy page of no more than eight years came to lead her to the king. Clasping her cold fingers in his soft, small hand, he led her swiftly along dark passages and up silent stairways to the most secret chamber in the castle. The only sound to be heard as they passed along the corridors flickering with torchlight was the soft padding of Morgan le Fay's leather slippers and the sibilant swish of her gown as it swept along the ground.

That night Arthur slaked his desire for this woman, loving her with the heat of his new-kindled passion, and ignorant that he was committing unpardonable sin. For him, this was a night of innocent bliss.

At dawn, before Arthur had stirred, Morgan was gone from Camelot, back to the kingdom of Gore and the security of her own castle. When she was certain that she was with child, she sent messengers on swift horses to take the tidings to her sisters. Without delay they rode at once to her castle where they rejoiced that the child soon to be born would be the weapon of Arthur's destruction.

Each day dragged by with a grim lethargy for Morgan le Fay, but when she felt the infant quicken within her, she grew impatient for it to be born. When her time was come, her sisters attended her and delivered her of a boy child. He was a tiny, frail mite who could barely cry, and so pale and thin that it seemed as if all his bones and organs were visible through his fragile skin. But Morgan le Fay suckled the tiny creature herself and soon he began to thrive. When it seemed certain that he would live, she named the child Mordred and wrote to Arthur revealing what had come to pass.

When Arthur received Morgan le Fay's letter he was distraught. Now he knew why he had been plagued with constant nightmares. Each night as he closed his eyes to sleep, all he saw were dragons and serpents invading a fertile land and then attacking and killing all living things. In his dream he battled continually against the invading beasts but could never overcome them. Finally, these creatures wounded him so grievously that he fell down dead.

Suddenly, Arthur
would find himself awake,
reeling in horror at what the dream
could mean. And in his half-wakeful
state he thought a pale-skinned youth of no
more than twenty years came to his bedside and asked him why he was
so cast down. But not knowing who the youth was, Arthur would give him
no answer, so the boy turned and left.

Now Merlin came to Arthur and warned him of the evil forces he had unleashed upon the earth when he had slept with his half-sister, albeit unwittingly, and begotten her with child. The fruit of this union would bring about Arthur's destruction and that of everything he loved if he did not destroy this abomination of nature. Merlin also explained that the unknown youth at the end of the dream was the magician himself who had shifted his shape into what Arthur's son would be, should he grow to manhood.

Arthur felt that somehow this vision had ripped his very future away from him, for if this child survived, what remained of his life but death? Now he knew how a trapped beast felt as hunters closed in for the kill. Fearful, but determined that he himself would not be destroyed, Arthur decided to counter the evil done to him by committing a greater evil himself.

Deducing the time when Mordred would have been born, he ordered that all male children born in his kingdom within a month of this date should be handed over to his men for slaughter. A hundred infants were ripped from their frantic parents' arms and taken to Caerleon where they were unceremoniously dumped on the top deck of a ship which was then sent unpiloted out to sea. (For all his bloodlust Arthur could not give the order that these innocent babes be put to the sword.)

Wracked with remorse, Arthur watched from the shore as the helpless babes lay naked on the heaving deck, chilled by the biting wind that blew the ship out to sea. Not long after its departure, the ship foundered on the rocks that littered the treacherous coastline beneath the castle at Caerleon and all the babes were drowned.

Meanwhile, the infant Mordred, the cause of all this carnage, was not part of the tragic cargo. At the first indication of danger he had been magicked to safety by his mother who would let no harm befall her precious son.

The Sword in the Lake

ARTHUR'S STRUGGLE TO ESTABLISH HIS RULE continued unabated as the minor kings who had first opposed him rebelled against his authority. But in those times, when a messenger could take many days, if not weeks, to deliver news, it sometimes seemed in the brief respites that peace had come at last. Yet, like the fragile early dewdrop that sometimes dares to show its graceful head too soon and is then destroyed by the treacherous nip of a late frost, so all reports of peace in Arthur's kingdom were premature.

However, news began to arrive at Camelot that one particular warring knight, King Pellinore, was wreaking havoc among knights loyal to King Arthur. He had pitched his camp close to the forest that was near the castle and rode forth from it to challenge every knight that passed who said he was loyal to King Arthur. Many noble and worthy knights had been slain in combat with King Pellinore, and finally Arthur knew that he must go himself and challenge this mighty adversary.

Meanwhile, a squire called Gryflet, who had recently come to court, was of an age with Arthur and was afire with ambition to be made a knight. Indeed, it was his wish that he should be the one to avenge all those knights who had been killed by Pellinore.

'Make me a knight, great king,' beseeched the freckle-faced lad. 'Knight me so I may conquer this unchivalrous foe.'

'You are too young for such an adventure,' said Arthur, who did not want to see this impetuous and courageous youth slain.

'I am no younger than you were, Sire, when you were made king,' replied Gryflet with an unmistakable determination.

After careful thought, Arthur agreed to dub Gryflet, but on condition that the newly-made knight swore to engage in only one course of combat with King Pellinore. So it was that Gryflet rode from Camelot, sitting proudly in his saddle, eager to meet with whatever adventures Fortune might throw in his path. His face glowed with pleasure as he cantered across the meadows from

Camelot, and soon he was near the edge of the forest. At the sound of his jingling harness, Pellinore, who was hiding just within the boundary of the trees, launched an attack. Sadly, the youthful Gryflet was no match for the formidable Pellinore; after one course he was forced to retire with serious wounds and only managed to return to court with great difficulty.

Arthur was enraged when he saw how the young man had been treated at the hands of the dishonourable Pellinore, and he immediately determined to ride out alone and declare his own challenge. When Pellinore heard hoofbeats which heralded another foolhardy knight approaching, he mounted his horse and rode out ready for a fight.

'If you be one of this milksop boy-king's knights, stand and fight,' said the knight with unmistakable irritation in his voice. 'I will not be governed by a boy that is only recently gone from women's skirts.'

'Stand your ground, for I am that king whose knights you have so churlishly destroyed. Make ready to fight me now instead,' called out King Arthur.

Immediately the two knights fell into a ferocious contest. Pellinore was indeed a fearsome opponent and it was not long before his sword cut right through the steel of Arthur's helmet, leaving him with a gaping wound to his forehead. The barely conscious Arthur lay slumped against a tree trunk, his sword – the very sword that he had drawn from the stone – lay broken in three pieces on the ground. Now Pellinore moved in for the *coup de grâce*.

Always watchful of any danger to the young king, Merlin had followed closely to see what ensued, for he knew well the great fighting prowess of Pellinore. Seeing the danger posed to Arthur, Merlin rapidly invoked his magic

power to create an obscuring cloud over Pellinore's head, causing the warrior king to slip to the ground in a deep and magic sleep.

Turning again to Arthur, Merlin was distressed to see how badly he had been hurt. Lifting him gently in his arms so as not to cause him any further hurt, he took him deep into the forest to the cave of a hermit who had great healing powers. Over many days the injured Arthur did not once wake as his wound closed and his body healed. Then one morning he awoke and felt himself fully recovered. Indeed, he would not have believed in his wound had he not had a scar to prove it.

'Hurry, Arthur, for we still have far to go,' said Merlin, urging the young man to mount one of the horses which were waiting for them outside the hermit's cave. And so, without further delay, they rode off, travelling for many days through unknown forests. Arthur did not ask where Merlin was leading him for he knew that the wizard would explain all when the time was right. Yet as he rode, he seemed to hear unseen voices whispering as gently as the wind through the leafy branches of the trees: 'Arthur is coming. Arthur is coming'.

On and on they rode through both day and night until, on the fourth day, it seemed as if they had passed into another country where the air was sweet and seemed to fill them with an inner peacefulness. Arthur and Merlin had reached

a land of lakes, which stretched as far as the eye could see to form a glinting chain of still water. On the horizon Arthur could just make out a curtain of mist that closed off the land beyond. In places this gentle, seeping mist spread its damp tendrils out over the lakes, which were formed by the waters running down from the soft, green hills. Lush vegetation abounded in this place, and every flower, shrub and tree grew succulent.

They rode on until Merlin stopped beside one particular lake that was marked out from the others by the beauty of the water. A glorious haze seemed to rise from its still, glassy surface and in this floating mist Arthur thought he saw the forms of water nymphs dancing with a careless grace, but when he looked closer he saw nothing there. He felt entirely at peace in this place, soothed by an unearthly music which seemed to rise from the waters and mingle with notes from the trees and hills, so that the land and lake possessed a delicate harmony all their own. It was indeed a place of peace and renewal; and as the sun touched the softly-sloping green hills, the blue water and the golden bark of the trees, it was with a new and warming light that Arthur had never before seen. As he breathed in the pure air, he dismounted and walked to the edge of the lake, where he knelt down and cupped some water in his hands. Raising it to his mouth, he drank a cool and refreshing draught.

'Where are we, Merlin?' demanded Arthur. 'This place seems like paradise to me.'

'This is the Vale of Avalon,' said Merlin. 'Beyond that veil of mist and beneath this lake is the kingdom of the Lady of the Lake, and close by is the Plain of Camlann where you shall fight your final battle.'

But Arthur had no thoughts of endings, for this place spoke only to him of fresh beginnings. As he knelt by the water's edge, his eye was caught by a blazing brightness rising slowly out of the centre of the lake. Then he saw the miraculous sight of a woman's arm, ivory-skinned and gleaming green and gold as the sun glinted on the bright samite that swathed it; in her hand she held aloft a mighty sword whose blade gleamed bright and true. Arthur felt himself rooted to the spot. I must have that sword, he thought. Never before had he felt a greater desire to possess anything.

'It is your sword,' said Merlin, as if he read Arthur's thoughts. 'Go now and claim it. Beneath these very waters the Lady of the Lake's swordsmiths began to forge it at the moment of your birth, searching for the ore for its blade and the gold to incise its name through all the countries of the world. Go now, Arthur, and receive your sword "Excalibur" from the Lady's hands.'

Arthur saw a small skiff resting on the shoreline amid some bulrushes. Climbing on board, he rowed out to where the hand remained above the surface, guiding him like a bright beacon. Now the boat seemed to move of its own accord and soon he had reached the place. Leaning out of the boat, he grasped the sword by its hilt and at his touch the woman's hand sank smoothly beneath the water. Arthur grasped Excalibur tightly, then held it aloft so that the sun caught the gold lettering incised on its blade. And while Arthur marvelled at the sword, the boat returned to the shore where Merlin was waiting.

'Arthur, one day you will return Excalibur to this lake,' prophesized Merlin, 'for when the time arrives for you to leave the world of man, you will come to find peace in the blessed Isles of Avalon that lie beyond the veil of mist on the distant shore. And it is then that your sword will be returned to this lake, for you are the only mortal ever to be born who is worthy to be its earthly guardian.'

As Merlin spoke, the dazzling vision of the Lady of the Lake appeared, draped in a surcoat of gleaming green samite wrought with golden threads, while her long, rippling, golden hair framed her gentle face. She crossed the water to where Arthur and Merlin stood enraptured, and as she drew nearer they saw that she carried a sword belt and scabbard for Excalibur, fashioned in the green and gold colours of her kingdom.

'Remember, Arthur,' said the Lady in a voice both soft and low, 'when you wear this belt and scabbard you will never lose blood in combat.' Kneeling before Arthur, she fastened the belt around his waist, just as a noble lady would do when a prince is made a knight. Then she kissed him on both cheeks, thus marking him out in the eyes of her people beneath the waters and in the misty kingdom beyond as the finest king the world had ever seen.

Strengthened by all that had passed, Arthur and Merlin rode away from Avalon. Arthur proudly wore Excalibur by his side, and for the first time he was ready to take up the onerous duties of kingship; the hot-blooded and impetuous young man who had set out to fight King Pellinore was now returning to his kingdom a noble and wise man worthy of his crown. Once back at court, his faithful knights were overjoyed to see him again, for they had feared him dead. Arthur told them of his many adventures and they were filled with wonder.

Many times afterwards Arthur thought of the Lady of the Lake and of all she had told him. He longed to return to Avalon, but knew he must wait for the Lady's summons, for her last words to him were that one day she would ask a boon which he was beholden to grant her. And in his quiet moments Arthur longed for this time so that he might again relive the many wonders of the Vale of Avalon.

The Knights of the Round Table

The First Quest

WHEN KING ARTHUR'S EYES first lit upon Guinevere, the fair and gentle daughter of King Leodegraunce, he thought her the loveliest woman he had ever seen and wished to have her for his queen. But when Merlin heard reports of where the king's affections lay, he grew perturbed, for he saw too clearly the tragedy that would come to pass if they should ever wed. He had looked through the billowing mists of time and seen that Guinevere would one day betray Arthur through her adulterous love for his best knight and dearest friend. Forcing his vision further into this turbulent future, a pensive Merlin saw that this alliance would be the cause of Arthur's death.

But the king was blinded by love and deaf to all Merlin's entreaties as daily he became more enamoured. Guinevere's father had been one of the king's first and staunchest supporters, so Arthur was often a guest at his castle. Here, the young couple would sometimes meet secretly in a secluded corner, happily indulged by the castle's servants. Guinevere was wont to tease Arthur and call him her squire, for she would never let him take his new-found majesty too solemnly. She often made him laugh and in her company Arthur began to regain some of his carefree youthfulness. Above all else, he was determined to make Guinevere his bride.

When Merlin realized that he was destined to accept Arthur's decision, he went as his ambassador to King Leodegraunce, as was the custom, to ask for his daughter's hand in marriage and to negotiate her dowry on the king's behalf.

Guinevere knew that a high-born princess should always marry for dynastic considerations, so she had never expected to find love through any marriage she might make. None the less, she did not find Arthur unappealing

and was somewhat intrigued by this young man who was so like the squires in her father's service whose rough manners were briefly chastened by gentle feelings of love. However, deep in her heart, unspoken to all save when she was at prayer, Guinevere knew that Arthur was not destined to be her great love. Her dreams were haunted by a beautiful and unknown knight, and one day, she felt certain, she would find him.

Summer warmed the rich earth when Guinevere and her bridal retinue of knights and ladies set out for Camelot where her marriage was to be celebrated. The princess's grey horse picked its way through the verdant forest, the bells on its bridle tinkling in a capricious rhythm that was picked up by the minstrels who walked beside Guinevere singing love ditties with an infectious gaiety. Following in train were many wagons of baggage containing the valuable dowry which the royal bride brought for her new life as queen of all Britain.

Arthur was so besotted with his future bride and so eager for the marriage to take place that he had not sought any land as part of her dowry. However, King Leodegraunce had sent with his daughter a large round table which Arthur's father, Uther Pendragon, had given to him. This vast table was made of all the different types of wood found in Britain and could seat 150 knights.

Fearing that Arthur's supporters might seem meagre at so large a table, King Leodegraunce had also sent 100 knights to swear allegiance and serve King Arthur and his new queen.

Arthur was overjoyed with this fine gift and immediately instructed Merlin to seek out fifty knights worthy of sitting at the table, for he had a fancy to see it filled on his wedding day. However, although he scoured the country, Merlin could find but forty-eight knights who were brave and chivalrous enough to sit in fellowship at King Arthur's round table.

The wedding day soon arrived and after the marriage had been solemnized with much pomp in the great cathedral, the knights all gathered in the castle's great hall to swear allegiance to King Arthur and Queen Guinevere. Camelot overflowed with happiness and the land rejoiced in celebration. The castle was bedecked with colourful flags and floral garlands, and its ancient stones reverberated to the joyful sounds of singing and dancing.

The wedding celebration was a magnificent sight. At the centre of the festivities stood Queen Guinevere, far outshining those around her, resplendent in a diamond-and-pearl-encrusted surcoat worn over a flowing, white silk robe. Her shining hair was coiled in a gold-threaded net decorated with pearls, while around her temples was set the priceless diadem that marked her out as queen of Britain. As she moved through the great hall, she resembled nothing so much as a swaying lily, pure and white.

At a short remove, a pensive Merlin watched the merrymaking, and when the great hall grew quiet as the company rested briefly from their exertions, he

spoke of the glorious age that all would now be witness to. Standing in their midst, he told of the many marvels that would soon be seen throughout the land and of the adventures that were at hand for King Arthur and his knights.

When he had finished speaking, the knights retired to the adjoining chamber where the great round table had been set. There they saw their names written in gold letters on the backs of the seats. Two seats remained unmarked and Merlin told how these places would one day be occupied by the best knights who ever lived. Pointing to the last seat, Merlin announced that it would be known as the 'Siege Perilous' or the 'Seat of Danger', for none but the purest knight who ever lived could take his place here unharmed; all impious people who dared would die for this unlawful action. When Merlin finished speaking King Arthur rose from his seat and signalled for silence.

'My fair knights,' he began, 'we have been told of many marvels today, and I pray that we are worthy of the glory God has seen fit to place before us. I vow that, from this time forward, all knights who sit here in brotherhood shall be known as the Knights of the Round Table. Each knight's worth shall be measured by his deeds of chivalry rather than by his estates or riches. I swear before God that from this fair brotherhood shall flow an awesome power of

good to protect the weak, to defend the just laws of this kingdom and to use our might for what is right before God and man. I vow that this order of knights shall cause terror to all evil-doers, and to that end I swear that the Knights of the Round Table will be ready to attack as well as to defend.'

'Amen!' cried all the knights as one mighty voice, rising to their feet to hail their king. The chamber resounded with an excited hubbub as the knights realized the great glory that was before them, then Merlin came forward again. He spoke at length of what it should mean to be a knight of the Round Table and how the fellowship was to be perpetuated.

To a man, all the knights rejoiced at being chosen for the Round Table and each vowed solemnly to return every year on the feast of Pentecost to renew his vow of fealty.

At this point Gawain, the king's nephew and eldest son of Queen Margawse and King Lot, asked to be made a knight of the Round Table. Thus, the custom was established that a man could join the fellowship only if he requested the honour and was then found worthy of inclusion.

King Pellinore, who had been won over to Arthur's cause and was now a knight of the Round Table, had great joy in seeing his son, Torre, also made a knight. Indeed, Pellinore had taken a brief respite from his lifelong adventure of seeking the Questing Beast – a creature half leopard and half lion – to attend King Arthur's wedding and to take his rightful seat at the Round Table.

The wedding celebrations continued on the following day; much food and drink had been consumed and the company began to tire. Suddenly, the sound of hooves clattering on flagstones was heard outside and into the hall bounded a white hart pursued by a white hound, which was in turn followed by sixty black hounds barking and lathering in their excitement to trap the creature. Around the hall the beasts careered, disturbing the somnolent guests. The white hart trembled in increasing terror, and when the white hound snapped at her hindquarters, she leapt high into the air, landing on one Sir Abellus and knocking him from his stool. Finally, the hart bounded out of the hall and streaked away on her slender legs.

Sir Abellus, who was not a knight of the Round Table, was exceedingly provoked at the incident and struck out at the white hound who came over to sniff him. Stewards rushed forward to shoo all the hounds from the hall, but Sir Abellus seized the white bitch in a vice-like grip and strode out of the hall.

No sooner had he left than in rode a dainty damsel mounted on a dappled white horse. Stopping in front of King Arthur, she slipped down from the saddle and she started to cry.

'That cruel knight has taken my sweet little dog,' she whimpered. 'You must right this wrong for he has taken what was not his to take.'

As she finished speaking, a mighty knight dressed entirely in black armour and mounted on a huge black horse rode into the hall. Stopping where the maiden stood, he reached down from his saddle, lifted her up from the ground and, pinioning her firmly across his saddle, rode off at great speed. Before long the maid's pitiful cries for help faded into the distance.

The chamber fell strangely hushed after these events, and King Arthur disappointedly surveyed his new brotherhood of knights who only last evening had sworn to protect all those who could not defend themselves. That noble sentiment was not in evidence now among his drowsy knights who were all suffering from a surfeit of merrymaking.

'Who will rescue this maiden?' demanded Arthur. Not a single voice answered, so it was left to Merlin to reply. He walked around the hall fixing one knight after another with his beady eyes.

'Do you bring dishonour on the Round Table even before it has begun? Will you let this infamous deed go unavenged?' he chided. 'Remember, no man can know what glory may follow such an unpromising beginning to a quest.' Merlin then chose the knights to follow this adventure.

'Sir Gawain, you are newly knighted, so you must prove your mettle in this quest. Find the white hart that began this episode and bring her back to court. Sir Torre you are also a new knight, so seek out Sir Abellus and bring him back with the white hound he stole.

'Finally,' said Merlin, turning slowly in a circle while every knight wondered upon whom his gaze would fall, 'you, King Pellinore, will bring back the damsel and the impudent Black Knight who took her away by force.'

Thus chided into action, these three knights made ready to follow this quest – the first adventure for the Knights of the Round Table. By late afternoon they were armed, mounted and ready to depart. Off they rode, soon leaving Camelot far behind. Their journey took them together over open country and through forests, but as night fell, they parted, and each knight went his separate way to fulfil his quest.

The first part of this adventure fell to Sir Gawain, who was accompanied by his hot-headed younger brother Gaheris as squire. The morning following their departure from Camelot, they rose at dawn, leaving the cave in which they had sheltered overnight. Having grown up on the wild island of Orkney, the brothers had spent many a long day tracking beasts through pathless brushland, so they had soon determined in which direction the hart had gone. They rode without ceasing until the forest thinned and eventually reached open ground. Ahead of them they saw a fine castle built on a steep hill and from the baying and barking that was carried on the breeze, they knew this was where the hart and hounds had run to.

Crossing the unguarded drawbridge, they made their way into the castle, but as they entered the courtyard they were confronted with a foul sight: a knight was slashing at the black hounds, and with each blow of his sword he killed yet another of these defenceless creatures. As Gawain looked closer at this unpleasant sight, he saw to his dismay that the white hart lay dead beneath the dogs' black bodies, her delicate white coat spotted with blood and her open eyes betraying the terror of her final agony.

'You have killed my darling beast,' wept the knight, as he continued to slay the hounds. 'You have killed the hart my darling lady gave me. For this you will feel the cold, sharp steel of my blade. You will have no mercy from me,' cried the bereft knight. Soon the castle's courtyard was spattered with the hounds' blood, while their pathetic bodies lay piled on top of each other.

'Why do you slay these defenceless creatures?' shouted an enraged Gawain. ' They only follow where their instinct leads them.'

'I choose how I take my vengeance,' said the knight with unmistakable arrogance. 'And if I so choose, I may take vengeance on you, too.' So saying, he turned on Gawain and the two knights fought a bitter duel back and forth around the courtyard. Soon, however, the superior strength of Gawain started to tell and he had his opponent begging for mercy.

'Why should I show you mercy when you showed none to these dogs?' said Gawain, raising his sword to deliver the final blow.

Just then, a lady came running from a chamber which overlooked the courtyard and threw herself on top of the defeated knight to shield him. Unable to stop the swing of his sword, the razor-sharp edge of Gawain's blade fell remorselessly and, to his eternal shame, it cut the lady's head off. Gawain was appalled and sickened by this accident, for through it he had betrayed every law of chivalry. His squire Gaheris, realizing the seriousness of the situation, spoke to him quickly and quietly.

'We had best get away,' he warned. 'We can never be safe here after what you have done.' No sooner had he spoken than four fully armed knights appeared on the opposite side of the courtyard ready to do battle. Gawain blanched at the ferocious sight of them. He and his brother were rapidly surrounded and soon lay on the ground in peril of their lives.

'You will always carry the guilt of this foul crime,' said the slain lady's knight who was called Sir Blamor, who would have killed Gawain on the spot had not the other ladies of the castle interceded for his life to be spared. The brothers were thrown into the castle's dungeons, but were released when it was learned that they were from the court of King Arthur, for the knights of this castle were all loyal to King Arthur's rule. When they heard what Gawain's quest had been, they severed the white hart's head and hung it from his horse so that all might see that he had succeeded in his adventure. But to this was added another burden, for Blamor put the lady's severed head around Gawain's neck on a rope and bade him carry her dead body before him on his saddle.

When Gawain returned to Camelot and told what adventures had befallen him on his quest, the king and queen were much displeased at his unchivalrous behaviour. The queen declared that from this time forward Sir Gawain would

be the champion of all women and do them good service whether they be high or low born, rich or poor, fair or ugly, old or young. Sir Gawain swore that he would do so to atone for the foul misdemeanour on his first quest. He also swore to be henceforth always a courteous and merciful knight.

The next adventure befell Sir Torre as he rode in quest of Sir Abellus and the white hound. He had not ridden far into the forest the morning following the beginning of the quest when a dwarf armed with a stave emerged from the dense woodland. With no provocation, he hit Torre's horse full on its nuzzle, at which the poor beast reared up in pain.

'Go no further until you have fought with the two knights I serve who await you in yonder pavilion,' said the dwarf, and turned to walk away.

'Why should I fight with them?' asked Sir Torre. 'King Arthur has commanded that I go in quest of a knight who has stolen a white hound.'

'Go no further,' repeated the sullen dwarf, at which he blew a small horn made of bone which hung at his side. At once two heavily armed knights burst out of the pavilion, leapt on to their horses tethered outside and bore down on Sir Torre ready for a fight. Being as strong as his father, the mighty King Pellinore, Sir Torre was a formidable adversary and had no great difficulty in knocking down both these knights with two powerful thrusts of his lance. As they lay stunned on the ground, Sir Torre made both promise to go to Camelot and swear allegiance to King Arthur.

'Tell King Arthur that the knight on the quest of the white hound sent you,' said Torre. Turning to the dwarf, he said, 'I have no squire, so I would like you to ride with me, for you have served your masters well and you will do well for me too.' The dwarf agreed immediately, so they rode off together.

'I know where this white hound is,' said the dwarf after some little time.

'Then lead me to it,' said Torre somewhat impatiently.

They rode quickly through the peaceful forest until they reached a clearing where two pavilions – one red, one white – were pitched. The dwarf told Torre to enter the red pavilion and there he found the white hound sleeping peacefully curled up at the feet of a fair, slumbering damsel. Without hesitation, Torre scooped up the sleeping dog and walked rapidly out of the tent. However, no sooner was the dog in his arms than the lady awoke sensing that some mishap was afoot.

'Don't take my dog, you thief, return it at once. Help! Thief!' she cried.

From the other pavilion strode none other than Sir Abellus to defend the damsel. He told Torre how the lady who had ridden into Camelot had no right to own the dog as this sweet lady had owned it since it was a puppy.

Torre was somewhat confused as to whom he should believe, and matters were made worse when Abellus tore the hound from his hands, leapt on his horse and charged off into the forest. Without a moment's delay, Torre followed him along the path he had cut through the trees and soon caught up with this oddly behaved knight.

'Return the hound to me,' demanded Torre.

'Never,' retorted Abellus.

'Then fight for it,' challenged Torre.

The two knights jousted, fighting as ferociously as two lions to decide who is to be leader of the pride. Filled with youthful vigour, Torre began to feel his advantage; he struck a powerful blow that toppled Abellus to the ground, but to Torre's exasperation the older knight would still not yield. At that moment a sorrowful damsel mounted on a palfrey rode out of the forest and approached where Torre stood over the fallen Abellus.

'Fair sir,' she cried, 'justice demands that you cut off this knight's head.'

'Cut off his head?' queried Torre.

'Yes,' said the maiden, tears streaming down her pale cheeks. 'He killed my innocent brother but two hours ago.'

As if in admission of his guilt, Abellus grew suddenly cowed and took cover in the nearby undergrowh. Torre pursued him at once and it was only a few minutes before he had cornered Abellus and once more he knocked him to the ground, this time placing a foot on his breastplate to keep him pinioned.

'Should I really cut off his head?' asked Torre, turning to the maiden.

'Yes,' she replied without hesitation. 'My brother begged for mercy but this dog only laughed in his face before slaying him in front of my eyes.'

Torre did as she asked. So grateful was the young woman that she invited the hungry and fatigued Torre to her castle where he was made most welcome by her aged husband whose frailty had made him powerless to avenge her brother's death.

Next morning Torre returned to Camelot where he recounted his adventures to the king and queen. They were exceedingly proud of this new-made knight; he had proved himself a worthy son of Pellinore, even though born out of wedlock. To reward his valour, the king and queen gave him lands and gold as befitted a knight of his noble blood.

The final part of the quest involved King Pellinore in finding the abducted damsel and the Black Knight. Not long after leaving Camelot, his journey took him past a distressed lady who was nursing a sorely wounded knight in her arms.

'Help us, great knight, for my sweet lord is near dying,' beseeched the grief-stricken lady. But Pellinore would not linger.

'Madam, I have no time to help you for I follow a quest for King Arthur,' he said as he rode by. So preoccupied was he with his task for the Round Table that he was careless of his knightly duty to help this damsel in distress.

Pellinore journeyed on and it was not long before he heard the sound of fighting close by – the familiar clash of sword on chainmail. He spurred his horse forward, anxious not to miss an opportunity for combat, as he was keen to test his knightly mettle. Drawing nearer to the fighting and peering through the trees, he saw that one of the combatants was the Black Knight himself. Hardly able to believe his good fortune, he then saw the damsel he was seeking. She was standing beneath the trees a little way off and shouting encouragement to the Black Knight's opponent.

This adversary was a marvel to behold, for he was dressed from top to toe in green armour. Yet it was not the green of the soft, mossy ground nor the leaves on the trees. His armour gleamed strangely with a watery hue, showing many shades of green and blue as the light caught on it.

Approaching the damsel, Pellinore asked, 'Why do you stay when you could run away?' The Green Knight, who fought with great assurance, answered in her stead.

'This damsel is my kin, and she is close related to the Lady of the Lake,' he replied. 'This perfidious knight sought to dishonour her, so now I am willing to surrender my life to defend her from such infamy.' As he fought on, he told King Pellinore how the Lady of the Lake, spying that one of her kin was in peril, had sent him a message on an enchanted breeze and he had gone immediately to his cousin's defence.

'He lies,' roared the Black Knight, as he tried with all his might to put the Green Knight off balance. 'I won her in fair combat at King Arthur's court.'

'Sweet heavens,' exclaimed Pellinore incredulously, 'I saw what happened and there is no truth in what you say. You burst into the king's wedding feast as we all sat at table unarmed and you took this maiden by force.'

The fighting had now come to a stop and both the Green Knight and King Pellinore looked disdainfully at the Black Knight.

'On my oath,' continued Pellinore, 'no one bore arms against this dog.'

'You claim to have won this lady in equal combat, Sir Black Knight,' stated the Green Knight, 'but how can that be so?'

Determined to be rid of the unchivalrous abductor, Pellinore drew his sword and cleaved the Black Knight's head in two. His quest now completed, Pellinore said he would be honoured to accompany the damsel wherever she

must go. But first they went to the castle of the lady's kinsman who entertained them as honoured guests. The following morning a much refreshed Pellinore set out from the Green Knight's castle to ride back to Camelot with the lady.

On their journey back through the forest they passed the spot where Pellinore had seen the lady cradling the sorely wounded knight in her arms. To his horror he saw that these two vulnerable creatures had been savaged by wild beasts and their bodies were scattered around in many pieces. Never on any of his knightly quests had Pellinore seen such a dreadful sight. As he buried their mutilated corpses, he was filled with remorse at neglecting his knightly duty and vowed that never again would he pass by any person in need of help.

The knight and the damsel then continued their journey, weighed down with sorrow. Before long they arrived at Camelot where Pellinore told of his quest. King Arthur was well pleased with the first adventures of his new brotherhood of knights and once more the court was given over to merriment.

However, Merlin took King Pellinore aside and revealed that the damsel he had refused to help was, in fact, his natural daughter and half-sister to the noble Torre. From that day forward Pellinore was a changed man who prayed daily for his dead child's soul and grieved that he had never known the young woman who was his only daughter.

The False Excalibur

Some time after King Arthur was deceived into thinking his abominated son by his half-sister had been slaughtered, he again welcomed Morgan le Fay to court unaware that she was still consumed with thoughts of how she might destroy him and thus gain vengeance for her father's death. Although as evil as the most venomous serpent, she still remained the fairest woman in all the land, and many kings and powerful knights had sought her hand in marriage. Finally, she had taken as her husband King Urygens of Gore, who was a fine and handsome man, rich and undoubtedly devoted to her. Unfortunately, his adoration made him weak for he was blind to his wife's evil machinations.

As this couple lay together in the darkest moments before the dawn, Morgan would whisper in her sleeping husband's ear, instructing him to kill Arthur and telling him how to accomplish this dread deed. Urygens, who was a good and honourable knight loyal to King Arthur, became increasingly perturbed at his treasonous dreams.

The seasons had changed but three times before Morgan le Fay could no longer endure the loyalty and love the people of Britain showed to Arthur, especially after he wed the beautiful Guinevere and founded the glorious order of the Knights of the Round Table.

Deep in the darkest dungeon of Camelot a hideous, red-haired dwarf was tempering the blade of a sword partly obscured by a billowing cloud of scalding steam. As the vapours momentarily lifted it could be seen that the blade was fashioned to exactly the same design as Excalibur. And, strange to tell, it seemed for a moment as if this ugly creature making the blade bore some uncanny resemblance to Morgan le Fay; in fact, the enchantress had shifted her shape into this dwarf form to strengthen the magic of her spell. She had forged a sword which resembled in every detail Arthur's famed sword, together with its belt and scabbard. All that remained was to unleash this weapon's destructive power on an unsuspecting Arthur and so bring about his downfall.

Morgan le Fay's beauty, which had ensnared many men, had fatally beguiled a French knight called Sir Accolon. Very soon she saw that he was the instrument through which she could bring about Arthur's destruction with no suspicion falling on her. Above all, she knew that Sir Accolon's devotion to her made him completely trustworthy.

Arthur's reign had brought a time of peace to Britain, but this harmonious age meant that there were no battles to distract the warlike knights and time often rested heavily on their hands. Their greatest pleasure during these times was to follow the chase, hunting through the densely wooded countryside for game that would feed the ever-hungry household at Camelot.

One morning, when the sun had lit the sky with a rosy light, a band of knights rose early, mounted their horses and streamed down the hill from Camelot excited at the prospect of a good day's hunting. Morgan le Fay had instructed Urygens and Accolon to ride close by Arthur's side and this they willingly did. The band of knights coursed through the open countryside, galloping as hard and fast as the swelling terrain would allow. Soon they were in the forest and Arthur, with his two close companions, had become separated from the rest of the hunt for they had chased off in the direction of a wild pig they had heard grunting and snuffling in the undergrowth.

As the three men pursued the pig, Arthur became determined that this beast should be their prize. Deeper and deeper they rode into the forest, each stride taking them further away from their companions. They rode at such a furious pace that it was not long before their horses were foaming and sweating, showing deep wheals on their sides where the riders' spurs had dug

deep into their flesh. Soon they could go no further until their mounts had rested, so all three riders dismounted and unlaced their armour.

'This is a fine thing,' said Arthur in exasperation. 'We are far from our companions and no one has a horn to summon them.'

'Well, I am pleased that we have had such a good chase,' said Urygens in an attempt to pacify the king.

'That is true,' said Arthur, regaining some of his good humour. When they had rested, the three men started off again, leading their horses on foot for they would have to find their way out of the forest before nightfall. They had not wandered far when they came to a clearing which opened on to a stretch of still water, and there was moored a small ship splendidly hung with many brightly coloured sails of orange and red samite. With some curiosity, the companions

made their way to the richly appointed vessel hoping to find food on board, for by now the three knights were exceedingly hungry.

Tethering their horses near the gangplank, Arthur and his companions went on board. Everything was well maintained and down below they found a main cabin whose wooden floor was strewn with large, silken cushions. However, although they looked from prow to stern, they found no sign of life – the ship was deserted. Feeling suddenly weary, the knights sat down in the fragrant-smelling cabin and it was not long before they all drifted off to sleep. The day quickly passed as they slept, the sun moving relentlessly to the west in the sky as the fowls on the water started calling to signify the end of the day. In the gloom of the cabin where the knights were dozing a light suddenly appeared and in glided three graceful damsels dressed in flowing robes of gleaming white samite and carrying lit torches in their slender hands.

'Whose vessel is this, fair maidens?' asked Arthur somewhat sleepily, but the maidens would give no reply, answering only with a light peal of laughter which sounded like the tinkling of small bells. Without uttering a word, the damsels gestured to the knights to follow them, and they were led into an adjoining cabin where they saw a table on which was laid a veritable banquet. Arthur and his companions needed no encouragement to partake of this food; waited on by the silent damsels, they ate well and drank deep. When they had completed their meal, each knight was led by a single maid to a separate chamber where each was assisted in undressing and made entirely comfortable in flowing silk robes. The knights lay down on soft, feather-filled beds and, even though it was but a short time since they had dozed on the ship's silken cushions, all three men were soon fast asleep. Little did they know that it was into a drugged sleep that they had now fallen.

After a timeless and dreamless sleep, Arthur awoke to find himself in a chill, dank chamber with heavy chains biting into the flesh of his wrists and ankles. As his eyes grew accustomed to the gloom, he saw that he was in a dungeon but had no idea how he had come to be there.

'So the merciless lady has bewitched you, too,' said a tremulous voice. Arthur turned to see a frail, bearded man dressed in rags who was also chained. He began to make out the shapes of many more men, likewise in heavy chains, which he now heard clank as they stirred to see their fellow captive.

'Urygens,' called Arthur, beginning to feel afraid. He heard no answer. 'Accolon,' he called again. There was still no reply.

While Arthur awoke a captive, Urygens was emerging from a drugged sleep to find himself cradled in the arms of his sleeping wife. However, he was filled with a deep foreboding as he looked at this beautiful woman slumbering by his side for he felt with a chill certainty that this magic was of her doing. But so great was Morgan le Fay's power over him that this besotted man's thoughts were not his own and he was powerless to act on this intuition. Sleep still hovered on Urygen's heavy lids, so despite his uneasiness, he gradually drifted into unconsciousness once more.

'How came you to be captive in this place?' asked an agitated Arthur of the old man who had first spoken to him. And the old man told how he was one of nineteen knights who, after being lured on to the enchanted vessel, had found themselves captive in this prison. Once there, however, each had been asked to fight for one Sir Damas in whose castle they were imprisoned. But, in turn, they all refused, for Sir Damas was known far and wide as an evil man who had dispossessed his brother Sir Outlake of all his inheritance; in fact, it was his good brother that Damas wanted the knights to combat. However, when Arthur heard this he thought that here was a way to win his freedom.

Shortly afterwards, he heard a light step on the stair and a damsel entered the dungeon to ask Arthur if he would fight as Damas's champion.

'I will,' declared Arthur, 'but only if these knights are set free, too.' The damsel promptly agreed to his demand.

'But I cannot fight without my sword and armour,' said Arthur.

'I shall provide you with all you need,' replied the damsel, turning to leave the dungeon. Something in the way she moved made Arthur think he had seen her somewhere before.

'You have been at Camelot, have you not?' said Arthur.

'No,' she replied, 'I have never left my father's castle.' But Arthur knew she lied for he recognized her as one of Morgan le Fay's ladies-in-waiting. 'Something strange is abroad in this castle,' he thought, and he sensed he must be vigilant for his own safety.

The damsel soon returned, bringing with her the very same armour that Arthur had worn while out hunting. As if at the start of some great tournament, Arthur's fellow captives hastened to arm him for combat. When this was completed, the maiden led the captured knights from the bowels of the castle and out into the sunlight where they had to shade their weakened eyes against the bright sunlight. Seeing how enfeebled and pale they were, Arthur became even more determined to avenge the wrongs done against them by the wicked Sir Damas. For his great service to them the freed knights gave their word as chivalrous men that they would go to Camelot and swear allegiance to the laws of the Round Table, but they were determined not to depart until they had given their champion strong and vocal support as he fought.

What befell Sir Accolon when he was taken from the enchanted ship? After a good number of hours he awoke to find himself lying precariously on the stone parapet of a deep well in a green meadow; if he had but shifted once in his sleep, he would have fallen to his certain death. As he teetered upon this abyss, he was filled with foreboding and wondered what had befallen King Arthur and Urygens. He dropped to the ground beside the well and stood to get his bearings. Suddenly he saw a dwarf, who was the Lady Morgan in disguise, come out of the nearby forest carrying in her arms a sword and scabbard that looked for all the world like Excalibur.

As the dwarf drew closer, Sir Accolon recoiled because this creature was the ugliest being he had ever seen. But as the dwarf looked up into Accolon's eyes, the knight found himself transfixed by some powerful enchantment.

'My mistress, Lady Morgan, sends you her greetings and asks that tomorrow you fight as her champion against the knight who will challenge you,' said the dwarf. 'My lady has instructed me to tell you that she loves you well and as a token of her devotion she sends you the all-powerful Excalibur as your weapon. She entreats that you wear this scabbard when you fight so that no blow can harm you.'

Accolon was overjoyed at Lady Morgan's message of love and did not care a jot how she might have come by Excalibur. Once more he was aflame with passion and ready to risk all in combat as her champion, and so great was his delight that he gave the grotesque little creature a resounding kiss. Morgan le Fay's magic had transported him to a meadow below the dwelling of Sir Outlake who had been wounded and so was unable to fight the next morning to win back his inheritance. Consequently, when Accolon arrived at Sir Outlake's house offering to be his champion, he was warmly welcomed as an honoured guest. However, Accolon would not have slept so trouble-free that night if he had but known with whom he was to fight next day.

Dawn had barely broken and the earth was still night-chilled as the two adversaries came to the field of battle and inspected their war horses who frisked and reared in anticipation of the combat.

'I have no sword to fight with,' said a concerned Arthur to his erstwhile fellow captives. 'Where is the maiden who promised to bring me my sword?'

Just before the appointed time, the damsel appeared on a fine white palfrey and in her arms she carried Excalibur secure in its scabbard.

'Good knight,' she said, 'I bring your sword at your sister's command. She bids me send you her tidings of love and obedience, and wishes you all good fortune in this contest.'

At these kind words the good-natured Arthur's apprehension towards his sister melted away.

'I knew you to be one of the Lady Morgan's waiting women,' said Arthur,

smiling at the damsel. 'Tell your mistress I send her my thanks and love, and we shall celebrate my victory when this day is over.' Then Arthur fastened Excalibur around his waist and for the first time since he had agreed to fight, he felt his confidence increase.

A horn sounded to mark the start of the joust. The two knights galloped towards each other, their lances set in their rests, and both were instantly knocked from their mounts by the force of their blows which splintered their lances. Both men struggled to their feet and the pages rushed forward to hand them battleaxes, the next weapon of combat. Lunging, hacking and ducking, the knights rained blows on each other until Arthur managed to knock the weapon from his opponent's hand.

Arthur and Accolon drew their swords, neither of them aware that Accolon brandished the true Excalibur. Both fought hard and strong but it seemed to Arthur that his opponent continually gained the upper hand. Arthur was perturbed and puzzled when he was gashed by his adversary's sword, for when he wore the scabbard given him by the Lady of the Lake he was immune to injury. These thoughts distracted Arthur momentarily, giving Accolon the opening he needed. With a well-judged blow, he thrust Excalibur through a join in Arthur's chainmail and a gush of blood showed that he had struck home. Arthur was shocked to be wounded and disturbed to find that none of his thrusts ever seemed to find its mark on Accolon. Some foul magic is at work here, thought Arthur, as he struggled for his life.

Meanwhile, within her watery kingdom, the Lady of the Lake began to sense that some unlawful person was wielding Excalibur. Rising from the lake on a mighty white horse, its harness catching all the colours of the rainbow, she rode with lightning speed to where Arthur was now in great peril.

The mighty struggle continued and Accolon sensed that he now had the advantage. Somehow Arthur rallied his strength and managed to sever the belt holding Accolon's scabbard; then he let fall a mighty blow on Accolon's head. Roaring in agony, Accolon rushed at his opponent with renewed vigour, raining blows upon his head. As Arthur tried in vain to defend himself, the blade of his sword broke and Accolon knew that victory was his.

'Yield, for I do not wish to kill a knight who has fought with such honour,' said Accolon with a commendable chivalry. 'Surrender, good knight.'

'I cannot,' said a weakened and disconsolate Arthur. 'I vowed to fight to the death and I would rather die than live with such dishonour.'

Having his offer of clemency refused, Accolon moved forward with some regret to dispatch his vanquished opponent. But as he raised his sword to cut off Arthur's head, the Lady of the Lake reached the scene of combat. Just as

Accolon's sword was swathing through the air, her lips uttered a frenzied spell and Excalibur fell from Accolon's grasp, landing at Arthur's feet. He was dazed to see another Excalibur and guessed at once that it must be the true sword while the one he had been using must be counterfeit. He moved forward to grasp the sword before Accolon could retrieve it.

In possession of his rightful weapon once more, Arthur felt a mighty strength surge through him. He charged at the unarmed Accolon, letting out a roar of anger fit to wake the dead, and struck a blow of such force that it broke open Accolon's helmet.

'It is your turn to die,' bellowed Arthur, more angry at his narrow escape from death than with the wounded knight. Suddenly, on looking more closely, he saw it was Accolon with whom he had started this adventure.

'Who gave you this sword?' demanded Arthur in an astonished voice.

The wounded knight told Arthur of the sword Morgan le Fay had given him and how she would have him for her paramour. At these words, Arthur had no more thoughts of the trifling feud between Sir Damas and Sir Outlake; his own kingdom was in jeopardy thanks to the evil plottings of Morgan le Fay.

However, Arthur's wounds now pained him so greatly that he could do nothing until they had been tended. He was taken by Sir Outlake to a nearby abbey where the monks cared for both wounded men but the hurt to Accolon's head proved so grievous that he died soon after. Arthur ordered that his corpse be sent to Morgan le Fay so that she might see the fate of her champion. Indeed, when the body arrived, this wicked woman had been making ready to murder the hapless Urygens for she could not conceive that her lover would be beaten when he fought with Excalibur.

As the bier entered Camelot, led in solemn procession by the Lady of the Lake, Morgan knew that she was entirely undone and could expect no mercy from her brother. Swiftly gathering her followers around her, she left the castle as if driven by some malevolent force. As fate would have it, she rode by the very abbey where Arthur was recovering from his wounds. When she dicovered this, she hid outside until dead of night, then entered Arthur's chamber intent on stealing back his sword. Finding Arthur asleep with Excalibur clasped firmly in his hands, she turned to leave, but then she spied the scabbard lying on a chest.

'If I cannot have the sword, I will have this scabbard,' she said with a hiss. 'Arthur shall die before he has its protection.'

Stealthily she left the chamber, rejoined her minions and rode at great speed through the night, holding the scabbard close beneath her cloak. At length she reached a stretch of water that glowed grey and ghastly in the misty moonlight. Taking out the scabbard, she hurled it high over the water where it fell and sank at once, hidden forever from all men's gaze.

A short time later Arthur awoke to the cloying smell of Morgan le Fay's perfume and was enraged to discover what had passed while he slept. Heedless of his wounds, he and Sir Outlake rode at breakneck speed in pursuit of the Lady Morgan, following her fresh tracks that were clearly visible in the moonlight. Soon they spotted their quarry.

Morgan le Fay and her band of knights were whipping their horses into a frenzied gallop, desperate to outpace their pursuers. Riding into a valley where many ancient upright stones stood, Morgan turned herself and all with her into similar stones to escape detection. Arthur and Outlake galloped around the valley in search of their quarry but could find no trace of them; it seemed as if the earth itself had opened to swallow them up. Eventually, when the king left, Morgan once more turned everyone back into human form.

For the first time Morgan le Fay was fearful of the king's anger, so she hid herself away in one of her fortified castles and spent several months in isolation. However, her rage against her brother showed no signs of easing. Daily she dabbled deeper in the magic arts for new ways in which she might kill him, as every day he drew breath, an extra pain writhed within her heart. She realized that any attempt on Arthur's life would only succeed if she could get close to him, and to do this she would have to make her peace.

Arthur was reputed to be a gentle and forgiving man - indeed, people often told tales of his mercy - so Morgan le Fay reasoned that when his anger against her had eased, she would be able to catch him unawares and kill him. With this in mind, she dispatched an innocent little maiden of her household to Camelot, instructing her to ask the king's pardon for his sister.

'Tell him, my dear, that I repent my past wickedness with all my heart and I am daily on my knees praying in penance for my sins against him. Tell him this cloak is a gift with which I entreat his forgiveness. Now listen well, little one - under no circumstances, for I shall surely know if you do, must you ever wear this cloak yourself. Remember this and swear that you shall do as I say.'

'I swear,' said the maiden, who was a little puzzled by this request.

This done, the little maid set off for Camelot, the cloak wrapped in hempen cloth slung over a mule's back. When she reached the court, she was shown into the great hall where the whole company of knights and their ladies were at dinner presided over by the king and queen. When it was announced from whom she had come, the chamber fell silent in surprise and expectation. Although in awe of this great company, the little maid acquitted herself well and did all as she had been instructed by her mistress. Finally, she called for

the gift to be brought forward. All marvelled at the beauty of this garment for never had anyone seen such patterning, such colours and such expert workmanship combined. At first, Arthur was not even inclined to hear what message his sister had sent but when he saw the cloak he began to think that perhaps there might at last be peace between them.

'I will accept this gift gladly,' said Arthur with a happy smile on his face.

'My lady instructed me to ask you to wear it so I might tell her how it looked on you,' added the maiden.

'Why, it will give me great pleasure to do this,' said Arthur. 'And when you return to my sister you must give her greetings from me and say that she is welcome again at Camelot.' Arthur rose and moved forward to take the cloak. But at that very moment Merlin, who had been sitting close by with the Lady of the Lake, jumped up and rushed over to where Arthur stood.

'This is a trap,' warned Merlin, sensing that the cloak must not be touched.

'Do not be deceived,' added the Lady of the Lake in warning, too.

'This cloak should not even be in your castle if it has been woven with the magic of Morgan le Fay,' whispered the Lady of the Lake into Arthur's ear. 'No one is safe until we know what witchcraft is hedged around it.' Arthur was sad at heart that such a fine gift should turn out to be so treacherous.

From where he stood Merlin was probing within the deepest recesses of his mind to discover what spell Morgan had weaved around this cloak. Suddenly he knew what it was and his mind filled with horror.

'Ask Morgan le Fay's messenger to wear it for we want none of her gifts here,' said Merlin, his tone betraying that he was not being entirely truthful.

'Let the maid wear the cloak,' said Arthur.

'I cannot,' protested the terrified girl. 'My lady made me swear not to wear the cloak under any circumstances. I dare not break her command.'

The girl's pleadings fell on deaf ears and Merlin moved towards her with the cloak coiled around his wizard's staff, for he would not touch it. The frightened girl took the cloak and put it round her frail shoulders, fastening the clasp with trembling fingers; the cloak swamped her tiny form.

'You will not tell my lady,' she asked forlornly. No sooner had she uttered these words than the cloak burst into flames, engulfing the poor maid. She screamed so piteously that none present forgot it to their dying day. So fierce were the flames that in less than a minute the damsel and the cloak were reduced to a smouldering pile of black ashes. Arthur knew now that he could never trust his sister.

When report reached Morgan le Fay of what had happened, particularly the fate of the innocent maiden, she grew even more determined to destroy

Arthur. But she knew that she must bide her time before trying again – and she could be a patient woman when circumstances demanded.

Merlin knew that he was soon destined to leave the kingdom for the last time. When he told the young king of his going, Arthur found the news hard to bear, for the wizard had become like a father to him. However, before it was time for him to depart, Merlin told Arthur of many prophecies which the king was to remember well in years to come.

The wily Merlin had fallen in love with the beauteous Nimue, Lady of the Lake. He longed for nothing more than to spend every hour with her but he knew that there would be a heavy price to pay for his passion. So besotted was he with the Lady Nimue that all at court thought he had lost his wits. Wherever she went, he followed, and together they journeyed through many lands where they saw many strange sights.

The Lady of the Lake was greedy for Merlin to teach her all the secrets of his magic arts, and this he did, hoping that it would make her love him in return. But she resisted all his lusty advances with many devious excuses and it was not long before the lovesick wizard was her slave. At last she had stolen all his magic and now she was ready to cast a final spell over him.

One day, as they were roaming through a leafy glade, Merlin was filled with a strange and sweet lethargy which forced him to lie down and rest beneath the shade of a blossoming hawthorn tree. Soon he had fallen into a deep sleep, and while he slept, bereft of all his magic protection, the Lady

Nimue wove a potent spell that the wizard was powerless to resist.

Suddenly, Merlin felt his senses filled with the heady perfume of blossoms and the buzzing of honey bees searching for pollen. In his heart he knew that he was drinking in these sounds and smells for the last time but he was unable to dispel the enchantment. He stood like a sleepwalker as Nimue took his hand and led him through the forest, saddening all the creatures who bid a silent farewell to the magician who had always been their friend.

Soon they had passed through the forest and were drawing near the calm and pleasant Vale of Avalon – that place where the glorious heroes of Britain take their final rest.

Lady Nimue led Merlin to the water's edge of the very lake where he had first come with Arthur when the king had received Excalibur from the lady's hands. As they stood on the shoreline, the waters began to ruffle and divide at the lady's command. Soon a path, approached by a flight of stone steps, was discernible on the floor of the lake. Nimue led Merlin down the steps to a

cavern sealed by a mighty boulder. At a wave of her hand, the boulder rolled aside to reveal a dank and murky cave, its walls covered with slime.

Docile as a lamb, Merlin entered the cavern and as he passed by Nimue, she kissed his brow. Without a backward glance, Merlin lay down on the cold, damp floor, the boulder rolled back across its entrance and the waters closed up once more. In this chamber Merlin may be found sleeping even to this day.

Sir Lancelot du Lac

ON ONE OF HIS JOURNEYS TO FRANCE, Merlin had travelled to the kingdom of the mighty King Ban, a loyal ally during Arthur's early wars to establish his rule. There, a war was raging between King Ban and King Claudas and it seemed that their feud would never be at an end.

Shortly before Merlin's visit, King Ban's wife Elaine had given birth to their first child but she feared for the safety of her infant's life. When Merlin came to look at her child, who had been christened Galahad but was always called by his second name, Lancelot, he comforted the baby's mother by telling her of the great fame and high renown this infant would win when he became a knight. Although gladdened by this prophecy, Elaine feared that she might not live to see these glories.

Lancelot's early life was spent in the safety of Benwick Castle, where his loving nature and goodness made him a joy to behold. By the age of eight he had proved himself a fearless and courageous child, prepared to dare all in accomplishing whatever chivalrous task had been set before him.

At last, it seemed to his anxious mother that Lancelot would safely grow to manhood, but then the war with Claudas worsened and the entire household at Benwick Castle was placed under siege. Although fortune had not marked down Lancelot's life for such a futile and ignominious end, Queen Elaine again feared for her son's safety, so she entrusted him to the protection of the Lady of the Lake. Remembering Merlin's prophecies that this child would grow to be the most courageous and glorious knight of the Round Table, the Lady of the Lake took Lancelot to her watery kingdom. Stopping up his ears and eyes with fairy glamour, she led him into the magic Vale of Avalon where he grew to manhood far away from all danger.

It was beneath the magic waters of the lake that Lancelot learned all his knightly skills and the code of chivalry by which a true-born knight should live. In all respects except one he grew up fine and strong: from childhood one side of his face was distorted, but such was his beauty that it made little difference. In later life he had no recollection of this lakeland time. In fact, his last childhood memory was of his mother lovingly enfolding him in her arms for a last, poignant embrace.

It was close by the feast of Pentecost in the balmy month of June, when the vegetation had become impassable in some parts of the forest, that King Arthur and a band of his knights were slowly picking their way through the undergrowth on horseback. Coming upon four squires carrying a wounded knight on a litter, the king rode over to see if he could help them on their way. Looking down, he saw that the knight had a gaping wound in his side.

'How came you by this wound?' asked Arthur.

'I cannot tell you that, good King Arthur, but I am on my way to your castle for I have been told by the Lady of the Lake that a man is coming to your court on the feast of Pentecost who can heal me of my wound.' So saying, the knight fell back on the litter, exhausted with the effort of speaking. Arthur and his companions were intrigued at this news, so they made haste to return to Camelot, impatient to see if the mysterious visitor had yet arrived.

The very next morning, after service in the cathedral when all the knights were gathered at the Round Table, the Lady of the Lake appeared in their midst and with her she had a gentle young man who looked of an age to be knighted. He stood tall and well-made with fine, large hands and strong shoulders which marked him out to be a mettlesome warrior. He was dressed in the watery green colour worn by those who were of the Lady of the Lake's kingdom and his head was lowered, as if in shyness. Looking closer, however, it was clear that he wished to hide his face which was twisted on one side. Suddenly, he tossed his head, flinging his hair back from his eyes, which shone with a clear blue gaze and took in everything around him.

When the sorely wounded knight from the forest arrived at the castle, he was admitted without delay and carried by his squires into the chamber. When his gaze fell upon the young man standing behind the Lady of the Lake, he began to cry out most piteously. 'Help me, fair young sir, help me, for your hands alone can heal me.'

Without hesitating, the young man walked over to where the knight lay and drew back the cloth that covered him so that all could see the terrible wound in his emaciated body. Kneeling down, the youth closed his eyes and looked lost in prayer. Then he placed his right hand gently on the man's wound. The injured man let out a deep sigh and when the youngman eventually removed his hand, the wound had been miraculously healed.

Astonished at this miracle, the knights listened enthralled as the Lady of the Lake told of the youth's life and his noble parentage. When she had finished speaking, she approached King Arthur and spoke with him privately.

'Arthur, I bring Lancelot to your court so that he may be knighted at your hand, for such was Merlin's last wish,' confided the Lady of the Lake. 'Merlin foretold at the time of Lancelot's birth that he would accomplish many great deeds as a knight of the Round Table.'

Having loved the noble King Ban, Arthur was overjoyed to hear that Lancelot was his child. Indeed, for many years no one had been able to tell what fate had befallen King Ban's only son, for the lands of Benwick had been razed to the ground by King Claudas's besieging army. Arthur looked closely at Lancelot and saw Ban's features clearly imprinted on his face in the bright blue of his eyes and the set of his jaw. The king was further impressed at how the great prophecies concerning him sat so lightly upon the young man's shoulders, so he immediately agreed to dub Lancelot a knight.

That same night Lancelot kept vigil in the cathedral at Camelot in preparation for the most important event of his life. The next morning he was dubbed a knight of the Order of the Round Table by King Arthur and, as befitted a king's son, Queen Guinevere herself tied the swordbelt around Lancelot's waist and fixed the silver spurs to his boots.

While performing this task, the queen looked on Lancelot and realized that his was the face that had so often visited her dreams and that he was the man she was destined to love. The affection and respect she bore for her husband could not compare with the passionate feelings aroused by simply gazing upon Sir Lancelot. However, she kept these thoughts deep within her heart, never uttering a word of what she felt. Likewise, Sir Lancelot was moved when he first gazed upon Guinevere and he knew that he could love no other woman. Silently he vowed to serve her always in the name of his unspoken love.

Like every newly-dubbed knight, Sir Lancelot desired above all else to embark on his first quest, hoping for a great adventure that would bring him glory. However, King Arthur's recent victory in his war against Rome had brought a time of peace, and therefore inactivity, to his knights.

To alleviate the boredom and keep his knights in fighting trim, King Arthur decreed a tournament should take place after the feast of Pentecost. In this tournament Sir Lancelot was proclaimed victor in every joust, but despite the honours he won that day, he grew increasingly restless at court. If he could

not be a knight fighting in his king's just wars, then he was determined to be a knight errant, wandering at will throughout the land, meeting whatever dangers came his way and thus bringing honour to the Round Table. However, if the truth be known, Lancelot also desired to remove himself from close company with the queen, for he did not know how long he could keep his passionate feelings in check.

Eventually, with his cousin Lionel accompanying him, he was allowed to leave Camelot in search of adventures that would test his knightly mettle.

On the first day of their quest the cousins rode for many hours without meeting any adventure. As the day drew on and the June sun rose high in the sky, they became increasingly hot in their armour and sleep threatened to overwhelm Sir Lancelot. Spying the shade of an apple tree, he dismounted, unlaced his helm and lay down beneath the tree's welcome shade. While Lancelot slept, Lionel sat nearby guarding their horses. Suddenly, with a boisterous swishing of branches, three knights rode out of the forest hotly pursued by a fearsome knight on a mighty warhorse.

'Here is an adventure,' thought Lionel, 'where I can win honour if I defeat this mighty knight.' Taking care not to waken his sleeping cousin, he untied his horse and rode off in swift pursuit of this warlike knight.

The story now rests briefly with Sir Ector de Maris, natural half brother to Lancelot. Sir Ector had ridden out of Camelot to find Lancelot and Lionel and join them on their quest, but try as he might, he could find no trace of them. An old man of whom he asked directions claimed to have seen the knights riding towards the castle of the powerful Sir Turquin. As Ector rode on his way, he came by a tree burdened down with a strange fruit. Stopping for a closer look, he saw the 'fruit' to be shields and noticed, to his consternation, that one was marked with the device of his cousin Lionel.

'Some robber knight has attacked my cousin,' he thought. As he approached Sir Turquin's castle, a massive knight rode out to engage Ector in fierce combat. The two knights bore down on each other at speed with their swords drawn and they met with a stinging crash that filled the air. Despite his bold defence, Sir Ector was soon overcome by his powerful opponent, who turned out to be Sir Turquin himself. Judging that Ector had fought bravely and with honour, he decided to spare his life, but threw him into the castle's dungeon. Here he found scores of other knights, among them his cousin Lionel, who had also been defeated by Sir Turquin.

'What are you doing here, cousin?' said Sir Lionel in astonishment.

'I could ask the same of you,' retorted Sir Ector at once. They both fell to wondering what had befallen Sir Lancelot, for they knew he was the only knight in the world who could defeat the mighty Sir Turquin.

Meanwhile, Sir Lancelot continued to slumber beneath the apple tree. As he slept, four queens rode by, shaded from the bright sun by a wide and gaily painted canopy. As they passed, they looked closely at the beautiful young knight and each desired to make him her own.

'I will put a spell on this sweet knight so we may carry him to my castle,' said Morgan le Fay, who was one of the four queens. 'When he wakes he will choose one of us to be his love.'

Highly amused and finding this adventure a great diversion, all the women agreed to the idea, so the sleeping Lancelot was transported by magic to Morgan le Fay's dungeon. As soon as Lancelot awoke, he knew he was the victim of some witchcraft and wondered where this adventure would lead. He could not continue on his quest if held captive here, so all his thoughts were turned towards escape. When the four queens learnt that their captive had awoken, they went down to the dungeon to explain their plan.

'Which of us is to be your lover?' asked the Queen of the Outer Isles, simpering and preening before him. 'We all like you well but we are generous enough to let you choose whichever one of us you most desire.'

Lancelot was repelled when he saw to what end this adventure had led him. If he stayed in this dungeon until the end of time, he would never love any one of these queens. He would rather die than succumb to the dishonour these women intended.

The queens could not believe his response.

'You will be skinned alive,' promised one.

'The queen will be tortured before your eyes,' said another, for Lancelot's devotion to the queen had been immediately apparent to all at court.

'Ten newborn infants will be boiled in oil before you,' threatened the third.

'A pestilence will strike the court of Camelot,' said Morgan le Fay.

Lancelot did not doubt that the queens could bring these terrible deeds to pass, but none of their threats made him weaken in his resolve to deny their foul desire. Cast back into the dungeon, he agonized about his predicament.

Some time later Lancelot heard a light tread on the stone steps that led down to his dungeon and saw a flickering flame outside his door. Through the gloom he heard a key being turned and in came a tiny maiden.

'I abhor the way you are being treated, fair knight,' she said. 'No one should make so light of giving and receiving love.'

'Thank you for those comforting words,' said Lancelot with great chivalry.

The maid then promised to help him escape from the castle if he would do her a favour when she asked it.

'What is it you wish me to do?' asked Lancelot eagerly, for he longed to be gone from this dark, dank prison.

'Tomorrow, before the castle stirs, I will come and tell you what is to be done,' said the little maid, and with these words she quickly slipped away.

Early the next morning, before the sun had risen in the sky, the maiden came to free Sir Lancelot, opening twelve locked and bolted doors so he could make good his escape. She had also brought with her Sir Lancelot's sword and armour that she had polished shining bright.

'What service can I do for you in return?' asked Lancelot as he mounted the horse she had brought for him to ride.

'My father is King Bagdemagus,' said the maiden. 'Tomorrow he fights in a great tournament where he has been beaten so many times before by Sir Turquin that he has lost honour and the fortune that was to be in part my dowry. If you would fight as his champion, I know he will be victorious and so retrieve his lost honour and fortune.'

Lancelot was only too pleased to undertake this task and the next day he rode with happy heart to take part in the tournament. Fighting alongside King Bagdemagus, he won glory and gold, thus ensuring the little maid's dowry.

'I will tell all my fellow knights who are unwedded what a wondrously sensible daughter you have and how she will make a good wife,' said Lancelot to a happy King Bagdemagus as he rode off after the tournament.

Sir Lancelot wandered through the land meeting with many adventures. Reports of his deeds travelled far and wide, but as he carried no device on his shield, he became known as the knight with no name who overcame all evil men.

One day, as he was riding along a stream that ran through a thick patch of forest, Sir Lancelot met with Sir Turquin.

'Who dares trespass on my land?' bellowed Sir Turquin.

'This is the king's land, robber knight,' replied Lancelot.

At once the men fell into combat and fought without cease for two hours, neither one gaining advantage over the other.

'Why, you are the most worthy knight I have ever fought,' complimented the breathless Sir Turquin. 'I am honoured to be tilting with you. My name is Sir Turquin. And yours, Sir Knight?'

'I am Sir Lancelot du Lac. You are a brave knight and I ask you to free those knights I know you hold captive for no just cause.'

Sir Turquin paused to consider the request. 'If you wish it,' he replied at last. 'But they are only lily-livered creatures who do not know how to wield a sword compared with you.'

So it was in seemingly great friendship that the two knights made their way towards his castle when suddenly Turquin turned sharply to Lancelot, saying, 'Why, my brains must be grown addled for I am sworn to kill a knight named Lancelot who killed my brother. You are this knight, are you not?'

Sir Lancelot made no denial, so the two knights drew their swords again and fell to fierce fighting.

'To the death!' shouted Turquin, and Lancelot nodded his assent.

The knights fought long and hard for they were well matched, but eventually Lancelot struck off Turquin's head with a mighty blow.

Once he had regained his composure, Lancelot made his way to Turquin's castle where he freed all the captive knights, including Lionel and Ector. After much merrymaking at their newly found freedom, all the knights promised to be at Camelot by next Pentecost to swear allegiance to King Arthur and his glorious order of the Knights of the Round Table.

On his travels once more, Lancelot met with many strange adventures and saved numerous damsels who were being terrorized by wicked knights. Reports of his exploits were carried to the king and queen at Camelot where they eagerly awaited such news, for they both loved Lancelot well and held him in high esteem. Indeed, he was hailed as the best knight in all the world.

Although renowned for his prowess as a fighter, Lancelot also had intelligence, and this was particularly tested when he found himself riding through Cornwall. For several days he had ridden slowly along a clifftop path, for a thick mist that rose from the sea made it foolhardy to venture off the track. It was a perilous journey and fearsomely cold as the spray-bearing, biting wind constantly lashed a tired and hungry Sir Lancelot and his horse.

Eventually, when the mist lifted, he saw a mighty castle, so he rode towards it hoping to find rest and shelter within its stout walls. As he approached, he saw two large, grass-covered mounds of earth rising and falling on either side of the castle gates. At first Sir Lancelot thought that he was seeing some strange vision as he had not eaten for at least four days.

Transfixed by the sight, Lancelot saw the mounds start to form recognizable shapes. Moments later, two giants stood before him. They were clothed in animal pelts and around their waists were strung the skulls of many dead men.

Weary and hungry, Sir Lancelot wondered how he could avoid fighting the giants, while at the same time thinking how disappointed all his admirers would be if they could see their reluctant hero now.

Only twenty paces from the giants, he could see their faces quite clearly and they did not look as if they were blessed with the wisdom of Solomon. 'Perhaps I can escape by outwitting them,' he thought.

At that very moment there rose a commotion on the castle's battlements. Looking up, he saw some damsels who shouted down to him.

'Ride away while you can, fair knight,' they cried anxiously. 'No one has yet passed unscathed by these two giants for they smash the skulls of all who try to run away from them. We have been held captive here in Tintagel Castle for close on twelve months. We fear the giants will never be defeated and that we will die in this place.'

Realizing this castle to be the place where King Arthur was born, Lancelot knew he would be unworthy to count himself a Knight of the Round Table if he could not free his king's birthplace from this menace. Dismounting his horse, he walked over to the giants, his heart pounding noisily in his ears.

'Fair sirs, I give you all good greetings on this fine day,' said Lancelot with studied civility. 'I trust the world treats you well.'

The two giants picked up some huge clubs the size of tree trunks from the ground, holding them as lightly as twigs.

'I much admire the sea from this vantage point,' said Lancelot in a friendly fashion. 'Will you walk with me a little way to admire it, too?'

The two giants were bemused by Lancelot, for no other knight had talked to them so courteously – indeed, most had ridden away in terror at first sight of them. When this happened the gigantic brothers delighted in striding after the terror-struck knights, picking them off their horses and squashing their armoured bodies between their fingers like children squashing beetles.

'We will walk with you, foolish knight, before we kill you,' tittered the giants as best they might with such deep and rumbling voices.

All three walked close to the cliff's edge. Knowing that the path on the edge of the cliff was treacherously fragile, Lancelot hoped that the ground might give way beneath the giants' combined weight – otherwise, he reflected, he did not rate his chances of survival very highly. Looking closely at the ground beneath their feet, he saw, to his great and silent delight, that the earth was already beginning to crack open beneath one of the giants. At this he beckoned to the other.

'Do you want to hear a riddle, my friend?' asked Lancelot.

'I do not think I will be your friend much longer,' said the giant with a guffaw. 'But tell it to me anyway.'

'Bend down so I may whisper in your ear,' said Lancelot. And as the giant did so, Lancelot drew his sword like a flash of lightning and with one mighty slash he pierced the giant's jugular vein and sent him over the cliff.

The remaining giant quivered with rage, making the earth quake as if in terror. Raising his huge weapon high above his head to strike Sir Lancelot, he suddenly teetered backwards as the cliff edge gave way beneath him. With arms flailing wildly, he fell over the cliff on to the jagged rocks below, his scream of terror scattering the seagulls for miles around.

Thus was Tintagel Castle finally freed from the peril of the two giants. The inhabitants streamed out of the castle, crying for joy and calling for the knight who had saved them. When they learned he was none other than Sir Lancelot, they said they expected no less from the knight who was known throughout the land as the most courageous and most fearsome.

The year had come almost full circle, so the time was near when Lancelot had promised to return to Camelot and tell of his adventures. Turning his horse eastwards, he rode for many days towards Camelot, his journey taking him through the Vale of Avalon. He remembered nothing of this miraculous country and the time he had spent there, yet he felt drawn to this place where he had grown to manhood. In fact, under the lake, unseen to him, all the creatures of this watery world who had known him as a boy gazed up in wonder at the knight they cherished so dear.

When Lancelot stood on the shore, he thought he heard voices singing out to him through the waters and felt strength grow within him. Later, as he left the lake and passed beyond this country, he felt renewed - filled with tranquillity and a sense of purpose to be the best and most chaste of knights.

On reaching Camelot, he told of his many adventures but breathed no word of the time he had spent by the magical and nourishing lake at Avalon. For the great services he had done, King Arthur loved his best knight well and held him to be his closest friend, as did the queen. Yet Lancelot's heart was filled with foreboding as to what difficulties his passionate love for the queen would bring about. When he had rested but a short while at Camelot, he took himself beyond the castle's confines, preferring to sleep in the open so that every breath he took and dream that filled his sleep would not be of Guinevere.

Sir Tristram and the Fair Isoud

WHEN KING MELODIAS OF LOTHIAN wed Princess Elizabeth of Cornwall there was unbridled rejoicing throughout his kingdom, and it was not many months before the queen grew large with child and her time for delivery drew near. One day, when the king had gone hunting in the forest, the queen found that her baby was about to be born, so she determined against all counsel to ride out and tell her husband of the great event.

Being a delicate woman, the queen found this escapade too strenuous for her and went into labour while riding through the forest. Helped by her waiting ladies, she was laid down under the branches of a sheltering oak tree and made as comfortable as possible for the birthing. Before long she was crying out in pain, trying to help her child into the world, and eventually a lusty boy was born. Sadly, the birth had taxed the queen's frail body and she was close to death. As she looked with wistful eyes upon her infant son, she instructed her ladies to tell the king that their child should be called Tristram, meaning 'He of sorrowful birth', for she would die in giving him life.

When King Melodias was told of his wife's death he grew mad with grief and could not bear to look upon his infant son or even hear his cry. Consequently, Tristram was reared by a wet nurse who cared for all his needs. When, at eight years of age, he was taken from this tender woman's care, he was entrusted to the protection of a wise old tutor called Gouvernal who grew to love the young prince as if he were his own son.

Young Tristram grew fair and strong and was brave and gifted in all he did. His quick wits immediately grasped whatever puzzle Gouvernal put before him and he was skilled in all princely accomplishments, being a fine rider, swordsman and athlete, and possessed of a natural chivalry beyond his years. Above all, he was gloriously gifted at playing the harp and created music so sweet that it would make the angels weep.

During Tristram's youth Gouvernal took his charge on many journeys to distant lands, and the noble qualities of the youth won him high renown

everywhere they went. Yet through all this time, Tristram's spirit remained untouched by any tender emotions. When he reached the age at which he might be made a knight, Tristram went to his father, who had grown proud of his only son with the passing years, and told him that he wished above all else to be knighted in his mother's land of Cornwall. King Melodias gave his consent for the young man to be dubbed by his uncle, King Mark of Cornwall, so Tristram set off on his journey, accompanied by some young noblemen from the land of Lothian.

This merry and high-spirited band of young men made their leisurely way through England to Cornwall, and on the journey all agreed to hide their true identity and pretend they were the sons of rich merchants seeking out trade. In this way, any glory they might win through chivalrous deeds would be the result of merit rather than noble family connections.

Some years earlier the Cornish king had been defeated in a war against King Anguish of Ireland and the tribute owing to the Irish had never been paid. Prompted by his nobles, the Irish king was now demanding his dues, saying that the matter could be settled through single combat with his Irish champion. However, if no champion could be found, then thirty children from the noble families of Cornwall could be sent in lieu to Ireland where they would be sold into slavery.

King Anguish's champion was one Sir Marhaus, a fearsome warrior who was brother to the queen. As tall as a tree and as strong as a dozen men, his piercing black eyes were sunk beneath beetling brows and his face was all but hidden by a shaggy mane of long red hair. So confident was he of his invincibility that he believed his great strength was all he needed to protect him.

Despair descended on the Cornish court for there was no man to match the Irish champion, and if King Mark did not deliver the noble children in lieu to King Anguish, there might be full-scale war again. The problem seemed insoluble, but then Tristram, who was newly arrived at court, stepped forward.

'Knight me and I shall be your champion,' he cried with exuberance.

'No, young man,' replied King Mark. 'Even though you might lose your life if we go to war with Ireland, I will not send you to certain death against Sir Marhaus.' But the king was gladdened by the lionheart of this youth.

'Sire, if I say I am Tristram, Prince of Lothian, and son of your dead sister Elizabeth, will you knight me and let me be your champion?'

King Mark was both astonished and delighted to learn that Tristram was indeed his nephew, and thus even more reluctant to risk the young man's life; but as no other champion came forward, he eventually relented.

And so it was that Tristram was dubbed a knight and named the Cornish champion. King Mark presented him with splendid armour and a fine sword as befitted his champion and kinsman, then the court bade him a sorrowful farewell, for they did not think to see him alive again.

The combat was to take place on a small, barren island a short distance from the Cornish coast. Both champions rowed to the appointed place in small boats – Tristram coming from the land where many sorrowful faces watched as he left for this perilous adventure, while Marhaus rowed from an Irish ship that had brought him across the sea. When the two champions faced each other on the island, Marhaus roared with laughter to see the tender youth who was sent as the Cornish champion.

'Laugh now,' said Tristram more determined than ever to prove his valour. 'I wager you shall not do so by the end of our struggle.'

'Proud words, milksop boy,' retorted the Irish champion, and as he finished speaking he drew out his mighty, double-handed sword and whirled it around his head, tossing it dextrously from one hand to the other so that

Tristram could see he fought equally well with either hand.

'To the death!' roared Sir Marhaus, pulling himself up to his full height.

'To the death,' said Tristram in reply, trying not to be intimidated.

A long and fierce struggle now ensued, and on both land and sea all that could be heard was the constant clash of sword on sword. On and on both men fought for close on six hours. Tristram began to feel himself weaken as he had used his strength too freely. Marhaus, however, showed no sign of tiring, and was quick to take advantage of a brief lapse in Tristram's concentration. In a flash he thrust his sword at Tristram's body, piercing the unguarded chainmail and inflicting a terrible wound. Tristram slumped to the ground in great pain.

'You are dead,' crowed Marhaus as he withdrew his sword, causing even more pain. 'Nothing can save you now for my sword was poisoned.'

Never had such a violent rage seized Tristram as it did now. With a frenzied cry and energy from he knew not where, he let fall a savage blow to Sir Marhaus's head, which cut through the steel of his helmet. The Irish knight fell down dead immediately with Tristram's sword embedded so deeply in his skull that it took all the young man's strength to pull it free, and as he did so, the tip of the blade broke and remained in Sir Marhaus's skull.

By now, the poison in Tristram's wound was beginning to take hold and he could scarcely move, but somehow he managed to throw himself into the small skiff that had carried him to this island. Having no strength to row, he drifted on the tide and it was not until late the same day that his boat reached the shore and fishermen came forward to rescue him.

When Marhaus's fellow countrymen had no sight of their champion, a small band rowed from the ship to the island and there they found him dead. The air was filled with their lamentations as they carried his body back to the ship. Once on board, they changed the white sails to black, then set sail for Ireland with all the speed they could muster.

At the Irish court the queen could not believe her brother had been slain, and even as she prepared his body for burial she hoped to find some small spark of life in him. She examined carefully the mortal wound to his head and deep within it she found the tip of a sword's blade. Knowing that this fragment could only belong to the man who had slain her brother, she prayed to her gods that fate might one day bring this man to Ireland so she might avenge her brother's death. This dread secret she shared with her daughter Isoud.

The Cornish court rejoiced at Tristram's victory and King Mark ordered the most lavish feast in his honour. Those noble families whose children would have been given into slavery lauded him, showering him with many splendid gifts, the most magnificent of which was an embroidered cloak which depicted on its intricately designed folds the glorious story of Tristram's life. Others desired to bestow their daughters' hands in marriage on Tristram, so highly did they regard this young man. All the people of Cornwall were agreed that he was marked out for many more deeds of valour during his lifetime.

However, these tributes and costly gifts were as nothing to Tristram, for his weeping wound would not heal no matter what treatment was applied. Spells and magic chants were daily performed around the litter on which he lay, but they were to no avail. Day by day Tristram grew weaker and Gouvernal grew more concerned. He realized that the only person who could heal the wound was he or she who had made the poison. Yet, if the antidote were to be found in Ireland, it would require great stealth to obtain it, for the Irish would not willingly surrender such a thing for the man who had slain their champion. As Tristram grew weaker by the hour, there was no time to delay and this dangerous mission must be embarked on at once.

Gouvernal advised Tristram to sail to Ireland incognito. Disguised as a merchant called Tramtris, his sorely wounded state might encourage people to help him more readily than if he went as King Mark's champion.

So, Tristram was laid gently in the little skiff which had brought his wounded body back to land, but on this journey the boat resembled nothing so much as a funeral barque, for all the things he loved most were placed around him. There was his fine sword, his shield and his bow, while around his frail and stricken body was wrapped his prized cloak. Save for fresh spring water in a leather skin, there was no other food to nourish him on his voyage.

The sick prince's boat was pushed out to sea and set on the currents that would take it to the Irish shore, and the people of Cornwall prayed that he would make a safe landfall. For a day and a night he travelled on the open sea, so weak that he could not even stir himself to drink water. He was ready to surrender to whatever the powerful and whimsical sea might have in store for him. Sometimes the waves and the wind were gentle; at other times he felt the wind get up and the sea swell, but the motion simply lulled him to sleep, safe as a baby in its mother's womb.

On the third day out from land, Tristram felt the poison take a greater hold; his eyes began to dim and he saw strange shapes in the clouds above his head. Soon the whole sky was filled with a bestiary of strange creatures climbing steps up to a fiery heaven. These visions gave way to unconsciousness as the little skiff ploughed on through the cold, grey Irish Sea. Porpoises frolicked and dived as they followed the boat, intuitively knowing that the vulnerable creature it carried needed their protection.

Shrieks and laughter came from the sunny strand where some small children were chasing the rushing tide. As they scampered further down the beach, they came upon Tristram's boat which the tide had carried high on to the shore. Looking inside the skiff, they squealed in terror and ran back to their nurse, shouting that they had found a dead man on the sand. She and her companions rushed to where Tristram lay and saw that the shipwrecked man was still alive, if only by the smallest margin.

'He must be a rich merchant shipwrecked,' said one. 'See the riches he has about him.'

'We'll be rewarded if we save him,' said a second.

All agreed with this, so they went straight to a castle that stood on a rocky promontory close by. There they found the king's daughter Isoud and begged for her help, for she was known throughout the kingdom as a great healer.

The princess responded to their pleas and was happy to care for this courteous and handsome young man. Indeed, something deep within her moved as she came to know the merchant Tramtris better. For his part, Tramtris was touched not only by the tender caring nature of this princess, but also by her beauty which had brought many princes and knights to the Irish court to seek her hand in marriage.

Like many Irish women, Princess Isoud walked tall and straight with swift grace. Her beautiful black hair was coiled into thick plaits, her eyes were deepset and sparkling, her lips were red as blood and sometimes, when Tramtris looked upon her too closely, her pale cheeks flushed to match.

Tramtris watched with wonder as she dressed his wound, removing the soiled dressing with the lightest touch and devotedly helping him to recover health and vigour. It was not long before the charming and graceful Tramtris was included in many of the Irish court's activities, riding out to hunt and joining in their many revelries. He won greatest good favour, however, for the skill with which he entertained the court by singing and playing on the harp.

This situation might have continued for many a month had not the queen one day seen Tramtris's sword and noticed that the tip was missing from the blade. 'There cannot be another sword like this,' she thought, and took it to the chest where she had hidden the blade tip removed from her brother's fatal wound. The pieces fitted together perfectly. Did this mean that Tramtris, whom all the court loved as their own kin, was the slayer of her dead brother? At once she told Isoud of her discovery and her daughter was filled with foreboding.

Tramtris was brought before the Irish king and queen to give account of himself. He revealed that his true identity was Tristram, Prince of Lothian and champion of King Mark of Cornwall. Speaking eloquently and with feeling, he told how he had grown to love the Irish people and declared that in fighting for his king and country he had behaved no differently from Sir Marhaus. Tristram argued so persuasively that no one at court had the heart to blame him for killing their champion. The king and queen were only too happy to make their peace and were even moved to think that if Cornwall produced such honourable men as Tristram, it was futile indeed for the two kingdoms to be continually at war.

When Isoud first heard of Tristram's true identity she felt a little deceived, but then relief surged through her, for now her secret wish to wed him was no longer an idle dream – he had proved himself to be of equal rank to her.

However, now that Tristram was entirely healed of his wound, he knew that he was honour bound to leave the Irish court and return to Cornwall to tell of his adventures. The mutual respect between him and King Anguish made the valiant young knight anxious to be of service to the Irish king.

'If I can ever serve you,' promised Tristram, 'whatever the situation, then I shall be proud to fight as your champion.'

King Anguish was delighted with Tristram's promise and wished that somehow he could persuade this fine prince to remain in Ireland and marry his daughter. But he would not speak of these things until he knew whether Tristram held any affection for his daughter.

When Tristram returned to Cornwall it was as if he had come back from the dead as no one knew for certain where his voyage had taken him. King Mark welcomed him with great warmth but in only a short time he grew jealous of the high regard in which the Cornish people held Tristram. Eventually his envy was so great that he could hardly bear to have his nephew within sight.

Since his return, Tristram had talked ceaselessly of the fair Isoud and his love for her was apparent to everyone. Acting out of spite, the king let it be known that he intended to take a wife as there was now peace in his land and he needed an heir.

'I can think of no better bride than King Anguish's daughter. You say she is fair, and surely such a match would bring lasting peace to our lands,' said King Mark, looking closely at Tristram's face to see what effect his words would have. It was with warped pleasure that he observed Tristram's sadness.

One day, soon after King Mark had revealed his intention of marrying Isoud, two ravens flew over the meadow where the king was walking with his nephew. In their beaks the birds held between them a single long hair which was as black as the ravens themselves, and as it fell from their mouths to the ground it appeared to land in the shape of the letter 'I'.

'This is a good omen,' said King Mark, 'for you have often spoken of the Irish princess's beautiful dark hair. I must delay no longer in this matter, you must return to Ireland as my ambassador.'

Heavy of heart, Tristram set sail from Cornwall, but only one day out a great tempest erupted, blowing the ship off course. Making landfall near Camelot, he decided to visit the Knights of the Round Table and see if their glory was as great as reputed. As it happened, King Anguish of Ireland had just arrived in Camelot to answer charges of murdering in cold blood Sir Blamor, a knight of the Round Table who had been killed in Ireland. King Anguish's guilt or innocence was to be decided by single combat, but being an old man, he was in no condition to take part in such a combat.

On hearing this news, Tristram determined to fight for the Irish King and thus fulfil the promise he had made to render him service. In the single combat that followed, the young knight was victorious, but with delightful chivalry spared his opponent's life. For this great service King Anguish rewarded Tristram with any wish that it was within his power to grant. Remembering his mission on behalf of his uncle, Tristram asked for Isoud's hand in marriage

for the King of Cornwall, even though he desired it for himself more than anything in the world. King Anguish, too, had hoped that Tristram would ask for his daughter's hand, but he graciously agreed to the request and settled the dowry for the alliance. Tristram then returned to Ireland with King Anguish, for it was his duty to accompany the royal bride back to Cornwall.

Isoud was distraught when she realized what her future was to be and wished she had declared her love for Tristram earlier. 'If I had,' she thought, 'I might have persuaded my father that I should marry Tristram and not his uncle.' Meanwhile, still uncertain of where his loyalties lay, Tristram simply tried by all means available to delay his return to Cornwall.

When news reached the Irish court of a ferocious dragon that was laying waste to the surrounding countryside, Tristram quickly came forward and argued that as King Anguish's champion he should be the one to slay this monster. Wearing a good luck charm made by Isoud, he rode out to find the dragon's lair, and so far-reaching was this hideous creature's destructive range that it was not long before he had come to the land the dragon had claimed as its own. The usually fertile, green land had been burnt to a cinder by the dragon's fiery breath and the nauseous stench of its foul breath hung like a sickly cloud above the ground.

Courageous Tristram rode on and soon found the dragon's rocky lair. Stealthily riding near, he found the beast sleeping, its vast body heaving with snores and filling the surrounding air with further blasts of malodorous breath. Suddenly the creature awoke and reared up on its hindquarters to an awesome height. Holding his lance steady, Tristram rode forward and with one unswerving thrust, he pierced the dragon's heart, its scalding blood steaming upon the rocks that formed its lair.

Bearing the heart of the slain monster with him, Tristram returned to court where all rejoiced that he had freed the land from this peril. The earth scorched by the dragon's breath regained abundant fertility and on the spots where the dragon's blood fell there sprang up a hardy flower with flame-coloured petals that is known today by the name Montbretia.

Shortly after these events, a messenger arrived from the Cornish court with word that King Mark was growing impatient for his bride to arrive. Tristram knew that he could no longer delay Isoud's depature. The princess and her rich dowry set sail across the Irish Sea, well-protected by King Mark's nephew. She grieved to be leaving Ireland and her family, but she grieved more to be going to a loveless, arranged marriage - especially now that true love had been awakened in her heart. However, her maid and close confidante, Brangwen, had brought with her a love potion of the queen's making that Isoud was to drink to on her wedding night so that she might find love with King Mark.

The voyage was nearly over; Tristram and Isoud were hungry for each other's words and glances, but neither dared acknowledge the great feeling that existed between them. For days both of them had stood on deck, as motionless as statues, dreading the moment when land would appear.

As the Cornish coastline came into view, Isoud went below deck to change her spray-drenched garments in preparation for meeting the man she was to marry. Her face was drained of expression, her heart was chilled and her body numbed. Seeing the flask that Brangwen had been given by her mother, she picked it up and undid the stopper, hoping that a few sips of the drink would revive her. A moment later Tristram knocked on her cabin door and entered to tell that they would soon be making landfall. When Isoud saw that he looked equally chilled she offered him the flask to drink from, too.

When both had sipped the fateful liquid, it was as if the bolted shutters behind which they had both hidden their love were now broken down and the light of their true passion blazed out. For once they gazed at each other without fear, filled to bursting with love yet feeling entirely serene. The next moment they were in each other's arms, their racing hearts beating almost as one. Isoud rained kisses on Tristram's face while her delicate hands circled his neck and caressed his tender flesh.

Both were powerless to resist their love, for now it was compounded by a love potion for which there was no antidote, yet both knew where their duty lay. The next day a sorrowful Isoud married King Mark, but after only a few months she and Tristram became lovers. At night, while the king slept, the couple would meet beyond the castle boundary and give full reign to their passion. They knew that by meeting in this way they were breaking the laws of God and man, but they were powerless to resist. Despite the knowledge of almost certain discovery and inevitable death, both preferred to take risks than to live separate lives.

Thus the couple pursued their reckless love until a certain knight, seeking

King Mark's approbation, betrayed them. They were surprised one night beyond the castle's confines and brought to trial. Tristram was sentenced to death – he was to be hurled from the towering clifftops into the roaring, rocky sea below - but King Mark showed a warped clemency towards Isoud, revelling in the misery that the thought of her lover's cruel death caused her.

Tristram was left with no time for farewells. After the sentence was read, he was led from the castle, bound hand and foot and cast into the sea. However, by great good fortune he survived, falling into a deep pool, free of rocks. As the ropes that bound his hands worked loose in the eddying waters, he swam ashore and that night took passage on a boat bound for France.

He made landfall on the coast of Brittany, a place that evoked happy memories of his youth when he had travelled there with Gouvernal. Here he found shelter and once again his injuries were tended by the king's daughter whose name was also Isoud. This princess was known as 'Isoud of the White Hands' because of her hands' pale beauty. Tristram came to like her well enough and before long, at her prompting, he agreed to wed her. But on the wedding night, Tristram could not bear to love her as a husband should for he was fated to love no other woman than his Isoud who was captive in Cornwall.

When news finally reached Cornwall of Tristram's miraculous escape and his subsequent marriage, Isoud was driven to distraction - a source of pleasure to King Mark who delighted in seeing her torment. To rub further salt into her emotional wounds, he referred constantly to the joy Tristram must be finding in his marriage. However, Tristram was soon to desert Isoud of the White Hands forever and return secretly to Cornwall. Here the lovers were reunited once more and meeting in secret, finding joy in the passion that would always fire their love.

Tristram and Isoud knew that they would have to flee from Cornwall, but they were ready to endure anything as long as they remained united. Luckily, fortune smiled on them and they found their way to Camelot, where a compassionate Queen Guinevere, who knew the sorrow of loving without fulfilment, took pity on them. She pleaded with King Arthur to welcome them at court and praise them for the enduring bravery of their love rather than condemn them for adultery. Thus it was that the couple found a safe haven at Camelot. In time, Tristram took his place at the Round Table and became one of the order's foremost knights whose valorous deeds were only surpassed in their greatness by Sir Lancelot's.

Meanwhile, in Cornwall King Mark's hatred grew and he vowed not to rest until he saw Tristram dead. Consumed with a thirst for vengeance, he devised numerous plots against the lovers, dispatching assassins to Camelot to kill

Tristram and Isoud by whatever means were available, but these all came to nothing. Eventually, King Arthur grew weary of King Mark's behaviour; he saw that it was futile for an otherwise worthy king to squander his energies on revenge and bring such ridicule upon himself. Arthur therefore interceded with the Cornish king, declaring that his anger served no purpose and that he would win the respect of everyone if he made peace with his wife and nephew. This he agreed to do, perhaps conscious that, with no son of his own, Tristram was still heir to the kingdom of Cornwall.

Shortly afterwards Tristram was invited to return in safety to Cornwall to make his peace with his uncle. Feeling only compassion for the king and his doomed marriage, Tristram accepted the invitation, overlooking the possibility that his uncle might still wish to kill him. However, the very first night, as Tristram lay sleeping in a chamber that had been specially prepared for him, three armed men appeared from a concealed door in the wall and set upon the unarmed knight wounding him severely.

Left for dead, Tristram managed with superhuman effort to escape through the selfsame door that his assailants had entered by and dragged himself down the steep stone steps which led out to the cliff and down to the sea. Slowly Tristram inched his way to the shore where he bribed a young fisherman with the prospect of gold to take him far around the coast to one of his father's castles in Lothian. The youth agreed, albeit a little unwillingly, for he knew that rendering this service would prevent him returning to Cornwall while King Mark lived.

When news reached Gouvernal at Camelot of Tristram's whereabouts, the frail old man sailed at once for Lothian. Here he found Tristram near death and it soon became clear that only Isoud could save him. Gouvernal immediately set sail for Camelot where the distressed Isoud waited anxiously for news of her lover. On hearing of Gouvernal's arrival, she feared the worst, and he did indeed confirm her terrible fears. She was filled with remorse that she had ever been foolish enough to let Tristram return to Cornwall for she had felt in her heart that he could never be safe with King Mark.

Isoud and Gouvernal immediately set sail for Lothian, but their voyage seemed interminable as the ship ploughed through the gentle swell of the waves. Isoud's thoughts often turned to the first sea voyage she had made with Tristram, which had marked the beginning of their love. But now the screeching of the gulls that trailed the ship matched the torment in her heart and she feared she might never again see Tristram alive.

Before leaving Lothian to fetch Isoud, Gouvernal had promised Tristram that when the ship returned and was in sight of the castle, white sails would be hoisted if Isoud were aboard and black sails if she were not. Now, as they sighted land, white sails were hoisted and they jigged merrily in the blustering breeze. Tristram had ordered that he be carried to the highest point in the castle so that he might catch his first glimpse of the returning ship far out on the horizon. Despair gave way to joy when he made out the white sails, for he knew that his love was on her way to him. He willed himself to cling as tight as he might to the fragile thread of life until he had seen Isoud once more.

No sooner had the ship drawn close to the shore than a fast skiff was set down to row Isoud and Gouvernal to land. And so anxious were they to see Tristram, that both waded the last few yards. Once they had reached the shore they ran to the castle, rushing up the many steps, each one taking them closer to Tristram whose eyes were now dimming fast as his death approached. When Tristram saw Isoud, his weakening heart pounded with joy, but it was more happiness than his frail body could endure and within a moment his eyes had closed for all time. At this Isoud's heart broke too and she fell down dead of grief at her love's demise, her body sinking next to Tristram's.

When news of the lovers' deaths reached King Mark, he was filled with sorrow and deeply repented what he was now powerless to change. However, he decreed that in death the lovers should at last be united for all time, so they were buried in a single grave from which grew a wild red rose around whose slender and thornless stem a perfumed trail of flowering honeysuckle blossomed all year long.

Sir Gareth

It was Pentecost and many knights of the Round Table made their way to Camelot for this great feast day and to renew their vows of fealty to the glorious order of chivalry. It was the custom of King Arthur's knights that they should see some adventure before the feasting began. This year, as midday and the time for eating drew near, many knights were already gathered in the great hall their mouths watering with the delicious smells that wafted up from the kitchens. Many a man's thoughts were set on the succulent haunches of venison that would soon be eaten, but they had still seen no adventure.

'Surely a trifling incident will suffice for an adventure this year, Uncle,' said Sir Gawain to the king. Hunger pangs were beginning to make this already hot-headed knight even more impatient than usual and by now he was not the only knight of this opinion.

As the weather was overcast and the great hall had grown dark earlier than usual, the vast chamber was lit with over 1000 candles that cast a golden glow over all who were assembled there. A lively hum of voices rose and fell in the gathering, but all fell silent as a strange sight caught their eyes. Three travellers who had arrived at the main gates of the castle some time earlier now entered the great hall to join with all the knights' families and retainers in partaking of this special feast. On any other occasion three such rough-looking and dishevelled characters would not have been admitted but hospitality was a tradition on this special day. None the less, all present could not help laughing.

'Here is our adventure,' said Sir Gawain excitedly, pointing at the odd trio and happy at the prospect of soon being able to sit down to eat.

One of the three was a dwarf dressed in rags and he wore a very disconsolate look upon his face, for his clothes had been crudely cut down to size from very much larger garments. Next to him stood a reed-thin man who was nearly bald and gazed vacantly around the hall as if half-witted; everything about him looked insubstantial and he carried a pointless spear in his hand, as though attempting to play the part of a squire. The youth standing with this motley crew was undoubtedly of a different calibre. Though seeming fine, tall and strong, he could not have been more than eighteen years of age. His face was proud and his gaze direct, he had a straight nose and firm chin, and dark grey eyes stared brightly from under straight, dark brows. The only incongruous thing about him was his hair, which was a sickly yellow colour, much like the coloured tresses of certain loose ladies who were wont to distract some of the knights from their chivalric duty at Camelot.

Some of the knights who had already sampled the wine set down for the feast were full of great good humour and needed little encouragement to find amusement in the three odd strangers. For example, when the youth bowed towards the king with a great flourish, a half-eaten loaf of bread fell from inside his jerkin and quite undermined the grave formality of his greeting. The whole company, including the king and the queen, roared with laughter, and even the rather po-faced Sir Lancelot joined in the merriment. But with a grace and haughtiness that seemed to belie his appearance, the youth quickly picked up the bread and tossed it to a waiting greyhound who fell on it greedily. The youth then walked over to where King Arthur sat.

'Sire, I have something to ask of you,' he said in such a way that Arthur felt impelled to listen. 'Grant me three wishes. I will ask for my first wish today, and the next two this time twelve months.'

'Ask what you will,' said Arthur, for he considered this a most diverting adventure for the feast day.

'Give me food and lodgings here at court for twelve months,' said the young man.

'Surely you have a greater request than this?' enquired Arthur. 'It is such a modest wish and so simple for me to grant you.'

'It is all I ask,' said the stranger, adding, 'and I ask the same treatment for my companions, too.'

'He is but a beggar after food,' burst in the irascible Sir Kay. As the seneschal of all the kingdom and responsible for the smooth-running of the castle and its kitchens, Kay knew that it would be his task to feed these vagabonds and the thought irritated him greatly.

'I would swear he is no beggar,' said Sir Gawain springing to his feet, for he had been much impressed by the young man's demeanour and puzzled too, for something seemed strangely familiar about him.

'Yes, leave him be,' added Lancelot, who had also been impressed.

Sir Kay huffed and puffed with ill humour but eventually, with bad grace, he agreed to feed the boy for the allotted time. In his own mind, however, he vowed to work him so hard that he would more than earn his board and keep.

'Off to the kitchen with you,' said Sir Kay. 'You will soon regret that you ever came to Camelot looking for charity.' But the youth ignored all Sir Kay's slights and remained cheerful, even though he had much churlish behaviour to tolerate from this uncivil knight.

All too soon it became evident that the youth was not an experienced scullion; among his many mistakes, he dropped eggs and accidentally set free blackbirds destined for pies. However, he was careful never to eat in the kitchens where Sir Kay might see him. He would not give the seneschal the satisfaction of seeing him eat and thus the opportunity for labelling him a beggar who had come to Camelot only for food.

The youth had large, white hands, which had obviously never known hard labour of any kind, so Sir Kay called him 'Beaumains', meaning 'beautiful hands'. Through all these tribulations Beaumains never once lost his temper or answered back Sir Kay. Sir Gawain, however, always had a kind word for the scullion, privately noting that he displayed an innate strength and dignity in all he did. When he saw Beaumains' fine, large hands, he told him he would make a fine swordsman. Sir Lancelot also kept an eye on the boy and regularly tossed him a silver coin with which to buy food, clothes or other necessities.

The year passed quickly, and once more it was the feast of Pentecost. The knights of the Round Table met again in the great hall and waited once more for the traditional adventure before they would sit down to the feast.

Suddenly, a damsel mounted on a palfrey rode into the castle's courtyard in great distress, calling out to King Arthur and his knights to help her. The maiden was immediately brought before the court.

'Why are you so distressed, fair damsel?' asked Arthur with some concern.

'I am Linnet, a handmaiden of the Lady of Lyonesse and for many long, hard months now she has been besieged in her castle by the wicked Red Knight of the Red Laundes,' said the maiden, sobbing all the while. 'He says he will not lift the siege until she has submitted to his evil passion.'

'Sire,' cried Beaumains, rushing forward, 'let this be my adventure. Grant me my two other wishes by letting me follow this damsel and free her lady. Let Sir Lancelot ride with me so that he may see I am worthy to be dubbed a knight. I wish above all else to be made a knight at his hand.'

Everyone in the great hall listened to the young man's passionate requests in silence and waited to hear what the king's answer would be. But before he could reply, the short-tempered Sir Gawain had leapt to his feet.

'Are you such a fool to follow this quest?' he demanded of the youth. 'Do you not know how powerful the Red Knight is? Why even I who am one of the strongest knights of the Round Table was hard pressed to survive my brief encounter with him. Do you seek death at your tender age?'

When it became clear that Beaumains was not to be deterred from following this quest, Arthur granted him his wishes. The damsel, however, was none too pleased at this development.

'Is this your bravest and most chivalrous knight to rescue my lady? This ignorant kitchen boy who stinks of tallow and grease has no more notion of what it is to be a knight than an ant,' she fumed. 'What insult is this that you put upon my mistress? I did not expect such treatment from the wise King Arthur.' Linnet's railing continued, then she turned and stormed from the chamber, leaving Camelot in high dudgeon.

Beaumains' two companions, the dwarf and the thin man, had remained close by throughout this incident; turning to them, Beaumains took two silver coins from his purse, gave them to his friends and then dispatched them on an errand. They returned soon after, the dwarf leading a broken-winded old nag he had purchased close by the castle gates, and the thin man clutching some rusty old armour and a sword that looked in great need of cleaning with vinegar and sand. In front of the assembled company the two men dressed Beaumains in the armour with a tender courtesy that was touching to behold. But Sir Kay was having none of this ceremony.

'I forbid you to go,' he spluttered. 'If you do, I will come right after you and drag you back to such a beating that you will not sit down for a month.'

'I do not think your threat will make a deal of difference,' said Sir Gawain.

Everyone watched Beaumains ride out of Camelot accompanied by the dwarf who was mounted on a donkey that skipped behind Beaumains' broken-winded nag and nipped at its hindquarters. No sooner was Beaumains gone than Sir Kay bellowed for his horse, intending to ride out after his errant kitchen boy and drag him back by the scruff of his neck.

'Come back, you cur!' cried Kay. 'Come back before I drag you back by your ears.' And hurling further imprecations, he rode at speed from the castle, his shouts gradually fading into the distance. Sir Lancelot, curious to see the outcome of this chase, decided to follow at a more sedate pace.

Soon Sir Kay had his absconding kitchen boy in sight. 'If I have to fight him,' he thought, 'so be it, but I will force Beaumains back to the kitchen even if I have to knock him off his horse.' Placing his lance in its rest, he rode at full tilt towards Beaumains, but his charge was spotted and Beaumains was ready for the attack. The lances of the two men met with a thundering crash and both were instantly shattered. Sir Kay struggled to retain his balance but without success; he toppled over and fell to the ground in an undignified heap. To add further insult to his ignominious situation, Sir Kay's fine warhorse trotted over to Beaumains when he whistled for it. According to the laws of combat, the horse was now rightfully his, so he mounted it and rode off with the dwarf, intent on catching up with Linnet and fulfilling his quest. As for the fuming Sir Kay, he had to walk back to Camelot with a nasty dent in his pride.

From his vantage point behind a tree Sir Lancelot had witnessed all that happened and been highly amused to see the young man knock Sir Kay off his horse. Once again he pondered on Beaumains' honourable deportment and skill at arms, finding it hard to believe that the youth was lowly born.

Beaumains had not left Sir Kay far behind when he was subjected to another attack. This time, a knight clad entirely in black armour and mounted on a fine black warhorse charged at him from the dense forest, uttering blood-curdling cries as he approached.

'Take flight, cowardly kitchen knave,' chided the damsel Linnet who suddenly trotted out from behind a clump of pale elms. 'Now we will see how courageous you are. Do not be afraid, Sir Knight,' she called to Beaumains' adversary, 'your opponent is nothing more than a stinking kitchen boy who thinks he would be a knight.'

'Heaven be praised for your kind words,' said Beaumains ironically. Standing his ground, he calmly placed the lance the dwarf handed him in its rest. Meanwhile, the Black Knight was filled with confidence at Linnet's words and at once believed himself to be unassailable.

'So this is King Arthur's mighty champion,' said the Black Knight scornfully. Placing his lance in its rest, he rode towards Beaumains who was ready to meet his charge. They collided with a mighty crack and, to the Black Knight's surprise, his lance splintered against the stoutly held lance of Beaumains. Unprepared for such resistance, he was thrown completely off balance and fell backwards on to the hard ground with a crunch of metal. Sir Lancelot, who had been watching from behind some trees, smiled when he saw what happened, while, for the first time since she burst into Camelot, the damsel Linnet was speechless.

'I yield, mighty knight,' said the vanquished Black Knight a little breathlessly, for his fall had winded him. 'I was a fool to doubt your fighting prowess.'

'Thank you, Sir Knight,' said Beaumains gracefully. 'All I ask is that you go with any followers you may have to the court of King Arthur and swear allegiance to him. Tell him that the knight of the kitchen has sent you.' The two men clasped hands firmly in the knightly gesture of farewell, but before riding off to Camelot, the Black Knight unlaced his fine suit of black armour and presented it, with his horse, to Beaumains as trophies of his great victory.

'It was only by chance that you overcame this great knight,' said Linnet, mortified at what had happened. 'Do not think that you are now any worthier to defend my lady.'

'As you wish,' said Beaumains patiently, 'but whatever you think of me I am honour bound to follow the quest King Arthur gave me. Nothing you can say will deter me from this.'

At these words, Linnet trotted off into the thick forest, careless of her safety. Sir Lancelot again witnessed this exchange and was much impressed with Beaumains' conduct and dispatch of the Black Knight. He was intrigued by this young man who reminded him of some other knight he could not bring to mind, but now he simply stepped forward to congratulate him.

'Sir Lancelot, make me a knight, for I wish nothing more than to be knighted at your hands,' said Beaumains.

'I would be honoured to dub you,' replied Sir Lancelot, 'yet I am a little curious. You ride and bear arms as if born to it, and conduct yourself with noble grace. Who are you and what is your true lineage?'

'I am Gareth of Orkney, youngest son of King Lot and Queen Margawse, and brother to Sir Gawain, Sir Gaheris and Sir Agravaine. After all my brothers had come to our uncle's court, I was determined to win my spurs by my own merits rather than because of family ties. I have not seen my brothers for many years and I thought they might not easily recognize me, but I still felt

it prudent to disguise myself with this yellow hair,' said Gareth with a wide grin. Lancelot laughed heartily at Gareth's story, and agreed that his bright yellow hair did indeed look peculiar.

'Your single-handed achievement makes me even prouder to dub you,' said Lancelot. 'Kneel, Gareth of Orkney, so I may make you knight.'

Gareth knelt, raising his young face proudly towards Sir Lancelot, who drew his sword Joyeuse and brought down the flat side of its blade on the young man's shoulders. Replacing his sword in its scabbard, Lancelot bade the newly-made knight to rise, then kissed him on the cheek. Thus did Gareth make his entry into the most glorious order of knighthood.

'I salute you, Sir Gareth, Prince of Orkney, and worthy knight of the Round Table,' said Sir Lancelot. Gareth thought his heart would burst with pride at these words.

'One further request I would ask of you,' said Sir Gareth. 'Please keep my true lineage secret for I wish to win greater glory before I reveal who I am.'

'I shall do as you wish,' said Sir Lancelot, although he was impatient to tell Sir Gawain of his youngest brother's brave adventures.

Knowing that he had tarried too long and should hasten on his quest to free the Lady of Lyonesse, Sir Gareth bade farewell to Sir Lancelot, then sped off into the forest. He rode as if his horse had wings, leaping over branches and thick shrubs and coursing like the wind down narrow pathways, all the while following the tracks that showed where Linnet had ridden.

As he rode deeper into the Forest of Danger, it seemed to grow increasingly green and Gareth struggled to keep alert because he found himself becoming strangely somnolent. He knew that he must keep his wits about him or he would be courting disaster. Then, a little distance ahead of him, he spied Linnet.

'Not you again, kitchen boy,' she said scornfully. 'Have you not yet learned your rightful place?'

No sooner had she spoken than a knight mounted on a fine white horse came bursting through the trees with his lance set in its rest. This knight and his horse were attired all in green and he carried sharpened tips of stout branches as the device mounted on his green helmet.

'Greetings, brother Black Knight,' he called in a cheerful voice.

'It is not your brother,' retorted Linnet before Gareth had a chance to reply. 'He is none other than King Arthur's kitchen boy.'

'How came you by my brother's armour then?' said the Green Knight with menace in his voice.

'I won it in fair combat,' said Gareth.

'You lie,' said the Green Knight. 'My brother is a most powerful knight and would never be defeated unless he had been tricked. Prepare to die, for I kill all who pass this way from the court of King Arthur.'

With these words the Green Knight charged towards Sir Gareth, wielding a battleaxe which he flourished with great skill. At this, Gareth quickly drew the Black Knight's axe which hung from his saddle. In an instant, both knights were lashing out at each other, their battleaxes making a fearful sound as they swished through the air. Gareth fought fearlessly, grunting with the effort he put into each blow he rained down on the Green Knight. Somehow it seemed as if he had taken strength from the Black Knight, striking out as if a panther raged in his heart. Eventually, Gareth struck the Green Knight such a forceful blow that he was knocked right out of his saddle and hurled into the branches of an overhanging tree, where he remained suspended rather ungracefully.

'I yield, mighty knight, I yield,' said the vanquished Green Knight breathlessly. 'Forgive me for my churlishness. Spare me, I beg you, and I shall do you great service.'

'Why, I should be glad to,' said Gareth with delightful gallantry. 'Go and pledge allegiance to noble King Arthur and serve him alone with all your strength and loyalty. Tell him that the knight of the kitchen sent you.'

'I shall do that,' said the Green Knight. 'And I shall also take my thirty followers with me to swear allegiance to your king.'

This decided, Gareth helped the Green Knight down from the branches and the two knights exchanged pleasantries. Much to Linnet's chagrin, the two men soon became firm friends; she simply could not understand why the noble Green Knight should be so amicable to a lowly-born kitchen boy.

That night Linnet and Gareth were honoured guests at the Green Knight's castle nearby and over dinner Gareth told his host of his quest to free the Lady of Lyonesse. In reply the Green Knight told him that in order to reach that place he would have to pass through the lands of the fearsome Blue Knight who terrorized the surrounding countryside. Indeed, the Blue Knight's reputation was so awesome that he had struck fear into the hearts of even King Arthur's bravest knights, Sir Lancelot and Sir Gawain, who had both barely survived fierce jousts with him.

'If this is the case, I shall have greater glory if I overcome him,' said Gareth, his Orkney pride suddenly making him seem as arrogant as his brothers.

Next morning, when all preparations to depart had been made, Linnet once more began to goad Gareth.

'Now is the time for you to run away, scullion,' said Linnet, as she had often said before. 'You will surely be killed this time. Why, you have made me weary of this quest. Return with me at once to Camelot where I can find a true knight to follow this quest.'

Gareth, too, was weary – the continuous insults of this sharp-tongued maid were more than a little tiresome. Taking one foot out of its stirrup, he dug his spur deep into the flanks of Linnet's palfrey. The horse squealed and reared, then galloped off at high speed into the forest that lay ahead with Linnet holding on as best she could. Gareth roared with laughter as he watched her hanging on for dear life, then he rode after her in a more sedate fashion to continue his quest.

It proved a simple matter to follow Linnet because her path through the forest was marked out by broken bushes and trampled undergrowth. Now that Gareth's anger was spent, he took care to see that Linnet had not fallen from her bolting horse and was lying injured somewhere along the way. Finding no trace of her, he continued on his journey.

As he rode along, Gareth began to notice ribbons of fine blue silk tied round the trunks of certain trees as if to indicate a route forward. This could only mean that he was nearing the land of the Blue Knight. He followed the silk markings and soon came to a place where the forest petered out into open ground. Halting to survey what lay ahead, he saw an open stretch of meadowland on which were pitched blue silk pavilions embellished with gold that caught the sun and made a dazzling spectacle. It was a glorious sight as knights and their ladies, all dressed in blue, promenaded to and fro with white dogs on blue silken chains. As Gareth ventured closer, he saw that all the flowers scattered in the meadows where blue – clusters of columbine, bluebells and cornflowers all blooming together in defiance of their true seasons. Then Gareth spied Linnet.

'Get away from me, for I am most sore with your conduct,' said Linnet in her usual blunt fashion.

'Enough, madam,' said Gareth angrily. 'I can brook your insults no longer. I have served you honourably and there is no knight at King Arthur's court who would have treated you with greater kindness. If you so wish it, I will give

up this quest.' Gareth spoke so masterfully that Linnet was quite overcome and for once answered him with civility.

'What you say is indeed true, and I beg your pardon for the way I have behaved. Forgive me. Perhaps we can start afresh, as though just embarking on this adventure,' said Linnet with unmistakable deference.

'With pleasure,' responded Gareth.

However, the newly found harmony between Gareth and Linnet lasted only briefly, for the atmosphere of goodwill was rudely broken by a blue knight mounted on a fine charger who galloped up to them.

'Kneel before me in subjection, you who dare to disturb the peace of my encampment,' roared the Blue Knight.

'Never, except before the king I serve, and that is Arthur of all Britain,' replied Gareth.

'Then prepare to die,' was the Blue Knight's swift reponse.

Gareth immediately made ready for combat, but while he did so he noticed a narrow and fast-flowing river that nourished the meadow. Nearby, a giant weeping willow trailed its slender branches in the blue water, so the tree itself took on a blue hue. Looking closer at this odd sight, Gareth saw that the trailing branches held many shields belonging to the knights slain by the Blue Knight. At the sight of a new victim, all the Blue Knight's entourage hurried into the pavilions so as not to witness the contest.

The two knights fell to combat close to the river, the Blue Knight filling the air with his blood-curdling cries. Their lances met with a crack like thunder and both splintered on impact. Now the knights engaged in closequarters combat. They drew their battleaxes and wheeled and dived towards each other, each trying to break through the other's defences, but neither combatant seemed to hold the advantage for long. After what seemed an age, the Blue Knight tired of using his double-edged axe, so he threw down this weapon and dismounted his horse. Drawing out his double-handled sword, he flourished it and beckoned to Gareth to do likewise. Now they fought with swords, lashing, hacking and parrying with unremitting blows. Both men were now tiring but neither was prepared to yield, so the combat continued.

From a little way off Linnet was shouting encouragement to Gareth. As the knights fought on, they moved closer and closer to the water's edge and the sight of the macabre tree with its gruesome trophies was enough to make Gareth fight with renewed vigour; he was not about to become a nameless shield hanging on a tree as a memory to his failure as a warrior. Linnet's encouragement also gave Gareth strength and when he felt himself tiring, he looked in her direction and returned to the fight with increased energy. At last,

from the very core of his being, he somehow found the strength to topple the Blue Knight into the river.

Weighed down by his armour, the Blue Knight sank rapidly to the bottom of the water leaving only a small stream of bubbles which quickly dissolved on the surface. Gareth considered that the contest had been well-fought and evenly matched, so he did not wish to see his valiant opponent die so ignominiously. Wading into the swift-flowing river, but staying as close to the bank as he could, he saw where the Blue Knight lay under the water. Using his last reserve of energy, he lifted the heavy knight and dragged him to the bank where he unlaced his helmet so that the Blue Knight might breathe. Both men, completely exhausted, lay motionless on the bank until they began to feel recovered. Then Linnet and the Blue Knight's supporters cautiously ventured over to them and carried the two exhausted warriors to a large pavilion where their wounds were cleaned and dressed.

'Tonight you will honour me by dining here,' said the Blue Knight.

He was, in fact, well pleased that he had at last met with a knight who was more than a match for him in combat. He turned out to be a delightful host who saw to all his guests' desires and he promised Gareth to go at once to Camelot with his 500 followers and pledge allegiance to King Arthur, saying that the knight of the kitchen had sent him.

When the Blue Knight heard what quest Gareth was following, he gave him wise advice as to how he might overcome the Red Knight of the Red Laundes who had surrounded the Lady of Lyonesse's castle with a great magic.

The Red Knight's power came from some supernatural source that made him invincible at first morning's light, but as the day passed, so his strength diminished, until by the setting of the sun he was as weak as a kitten. Having discovered how he might defeat this great foe, Gareth turned his mind to enjoyment, for it was many a day since he had been entertained so well.

That night, after having bathed and eaten, Gareth slept like a babe between fine silken sheets in the beautiful pavilion of the Blue Knight himself, a gentle breeze fanning his body. An hour past dawn, however, he awoke to find a beautiful young damsel in the tent and saw to his astonishment that she was entirely naked, her modesty preserved only by her long golden hair which flowed around her down to her knees. The next instant she slipped into the bed and lay down beside a startled Gareth where she quivered like a startled leveret.

'My father told me to come and lie with you, for he says you are the worthiest knight he has ever known,' said the little maid who could not have been more than sixteen years old.

Gareth was both concerned and excited at her behaviour. 'Is your father the Blue Knight, Sir Persant?' he asked.

'Yes,' replied the girl.

'Are you a maiden or married?' asked Gareth.

'I am a maid,' she said.

'Then it would be most shameful for me to lie with you and take your maidenhead,' said Gareth. At this, he wrapped a silken sheet around her nakedness and gently ejected her from his bed.

When the maiden told her father what Gareth had said he knew that here was one of the finest knights ever born, and he thought how he would make a worthy husband for his daughter Katharine. However, although Gareth liked the maiden well, he did not feel that her father's hospitality need extend that far. Indeed, his thoughts were more preoccupied with the final part of his quest that would lead him to the besieged lands of the Lady of Lyonesse.

The sun was well up in the sky when Gareth and Linnet set off for the final part of their journey. By late morning they had reached the borders of the land of Lyonesse, and within an hour they were in sight of the dread Castle Dangerous.

On their journey they had been accompanied by a dwarf in service with the Blue Knight and he had led them through the forest. Now Gareth sent the little creature ahead with a message for the besieged Lady of Lyonesse. Linnet told him where he would find a secret entrance to the castle, and his small size

would make it easy for him to escape detection on the way. The dwarf set off, but not without some grumbling, for he thought the task too dangerous for such a little man. But he was a wily old creature who had journeyed through numerous lands, including Orkney, so he recognized Gareth at once.

'You are King Lot's youngest son,' he said. 'I spent many months at his castle on Orkney and you resemble him greatly.'

Gareth saw that it was pointless to make a denial. 'I am indeed Gareth,' he confirmed, but swore the dwarf to secrecy, promising him a bag of gold for his silence and if he completed the task now set before him.

The dwarf found his way without difficulty into the castle and told the lady of the perilous adventures that Gareth had survived to save her from the peril of the Red Knight.

By now night had fallen, so Gareth lay down to rest. When the next morning dawned, he ventured closer to the castle and saw columns of smoke furling up from the camp fires of the besieging forces of the Red Knight. As Gareth and Linnet picked their way slowly forward on their horses, they saw a horrendous sight that made them turn pale and sick; hanging among the trees, fully armed and their shields slung around their necks, were the decaying bodies of at least forty knights, the butchered victims of the Red Knight. At the sight of these Gareth felt his gorge rise.

'Take heart,' encouraged Linnet. 'You know how to defeat this foe.'

Riding on, they passed by a sycamore tree on whose branches hung a mighty horn of ivory. 'If you blow on this horn you summon the Red Knight,' said Linnet.

'I would far rather die in battle than at the unmerciful hands of the Red Knight who only has his strength through necromancy,' said Gareth. But summoning up his courage, he took the horn in both hands and blew a mighty blast on it. At this, all the soldiers in the Red Knight's army turned to see what foolhardy knight errant had dared summon their overlord to combat.

No sooner had the note died, than the Red Knight himself appeared, already mounted on his fearsome warhorse who champed at the bit to be away to combat. Two attendants buckled the Red Knight's sword to his belt and handed up his helmet. Finally, taking a weighty lance in one hand and his great shield in the other, he galloped out to meet the foolhardy knight who dared challenge him.

Meanwhile, the besieged inhabitants of the castle made their way to the battlements to exhort Gareth to victory where so many others had failed.

'Look - my lady sends you all good fortune,' said Linnet, pointing to a window high in the castle. 'She prays that you will be victorious so she may be freed from the Red Knight's wickedness.' Gareth looked to where Linnet pointed and caught sight of the lady, who even at this distance seemed to be as gentle as a turtle dove. Gareth hardened his resolve to be victorious for her.

The fiery sun was now high in the sky so no shadows were cast by the castle walls. A brisk breeze blew, scattering the wispy white clouds and ruffling the bright pennants on the besieging army's red pavilions. But more macabre by far was the sound wrought by this breeze, for it swung the dead knights' decaying bodies to and fro, making their rusty armour squeak with a grotesque monotony.

'Prepare to die, foolish knight,' bellowed the Red Knight.

Gareth bade Linnet to get away to safety, then the two combatants set their lances in their rests and charged towards each other. They came together with such force that the girths holding their saddles secure burst open and both knights were thrown to the ground with a mighty clatter. Both men were badly winded and for a while they could only lay on the ground, stranded like upturned lobsters. Those on the castle battlements thought the knights had broken their necks, but then the armoured creatures began to move and drag themselves laboriously to their feet. Once upright, they drew their swords and began to fight anew, struggling for dominance like mighty lions.

On and on they fought for what seemed like an age, each man panting, bleeding and groaning with his wounds. Gareth seemed possessed as he hacked at the Red Knight, but neither held the advantage for long. Throughout this mortal combat neither man paused or called for rest; both knew it was a fight to the death. Each man grew wily in his tactics and each held his adversary in high respect.

Suddenly, Gareth lost his footing and slipped to the ground, at which an audible gasp rose from the castle battlements. His helmet had been so badly damaged in the fight that it gave him no protection, and as quickly as a venomous snake flashes its forked tongue, so the Red Knight towered over him and prepared to deliver the *coup de grâce*. Gareth seemed to have all but given up the struggle when Linnet shouted out to rouse him.

'See how my lady weeps to see you defeated. See how her cheeks are coursed with tears. Do not let her see you die,' urged Linnet, beginning to sob herself, for she did not wish to see her brave companion die.

By now the sun had moved across the sky and the shadows cast by the castle walls were beginning to lengthen. From he knew not where, Gareth found the strength to kick the Red Knight away from him, knocking him off balance and casting him to the ground, his sword clattering from his hand. Now the tables were turned and the Red Knight's strength began to seep away.

'Spare me,' he pleaded. 'Mercy.'

Gareth's thoughts turned to the many knights that had not been spared when they had been in just this situation and he was sorely tempted to dispatch the Red Knight on the spot.

'Tell me why you slayed so many fine knights,' demanded Gareth.

'I once loved a lady even more than my own life, who was lady-in-waiting to Morgan le Fay,' explained the Red Knight. 'When her brother was killed by one of the knights of the Round Table, I promised her that I would kill all knights from that order who passed my way. I vowed that they would suffer as much as her poor brother.'

'Spare him,' interceded Linnet. 'His cruelty was not all his own but wrought by the magic of Morgan le Fay who has vowed to destroy the Round Table and bring dishonour to all its knights.'

Many other knights present also asked for the Red Knight's life to be spared and when Gareth had heard their pleas, he judged that the Red Knight should go to Camelot and beg forgiveness from the families of those he had slain.

Now the wicked enchantment that had surrounded him was broken, the Red Knight showed himself to be a noble and courteous host. He saw that Gareth's wounds were carefully tended and that he soon regained his strength. Some ten days later Gareth was ready to ride back to Camelot where he would tell of his great adventures. But before leaving he wished to meet the beauteous Lady of Lyonesse whom he had rescued.

One fine morning he rode to the castle, but as he made his way across the drawbridge he was bewildered to find the portcullis barred his entry. He could not understand this action until the lady herself appeared at an upper window and started to rail at him.

'Go away,' she cried with just as much vehemence as Linnet had done at the start of this adventure. 'No kitchen boy shall pay court to me. Get you gone, you base-born scoundrel who plays at being a knight.'

Gareth was enraged to meet such a response so he turned his horse and rode away, determined never to think kindly of the Lady of Lyonesse for whom he had endured so many perils. 'I will wed Katharine, the little daughter of the Blue Knight,' he thought as he cantered away without a backward glance. But for all her harsh and hurtful words, the Lady of Lyonesse was much taken with Gareth's graceful good looks. Reflecting upon this, she sent her brother to find the dwarf who had first brought news of her rescue, and to bring him back by force if necessary. The lady was certain that this crafty creature would know more about her rescuer.

The dwarf was easily captured and brought to the castle, squealing like a pig on its way to slaughter. On arrival he was flung into the deepest dungeon. But as luck would have it, one of the Blue Knight's retainers had seen the dwarf's abduction and told Gareth, who set off at once to rescue him.

The poor dwarf was shamefully mistreated in the dungeon and it was not long before he had revealed Gareth's true lineage. Consequently, when Gareth rode up to the castle, he was bemused by the change in the Lady of Lyonesse's behaviour. Bedecked in jewels and fine clothes, her skin radiant and smoothed with many exotic unguents, she approached the astonished Gareth, the air around her growing sweet with some intoxicating perfume.

'Welcome, brave knight, have you come for your dwarf?' said the lady in honeyed tones. 'Brother, go fetch him, for I am sure the sweet little man wishes to be reunited with his master after such a long separation.' Turning again to Gareth and fixing him with a deep gaze, she said, 'You have done me great service in freeing my lands from the Red Knight. How can I ever repay my noble rescuer?' Sighing deeply, she continued, 'But you must know that I will always love you for this chivalrous deed.'

Although Gareth had great skill in arms, he had no knowledge of the game of love and was entirely captivated by the calculated lovemaking of this lady. The innocent knight immediately forgave her earlier ungracious behaviour, and it was not long before the couple were billing and cooing like lovebirds in the castle's arbour. Soon the lady began to hint that she wished to be with Gareth forever, and the young man, who burned hot with desire for her, believed that the love she declared for him was truly felt.

The affair between the knight and the lady would have continued apace had not the dwarf, who had suffered sorely from the lady's cruel wickedness, revealed her true character to the lovesick Gareth. Each night at a strictly observed time the Lady of Lyonesse went alone to her chapel to pray. Several nights after Gareth had been welcomed to the Castle Dangerous, he followed her there at the dwarf's insistence so that he might spy on her as she was at her meditations. The dwarf had chanced to see her here once before and it was a sight he would never forget. Hidden in the shadows, Gareth watched as the lady walked to the front of the chapel, but there was no altar or any religious artefact to mark it out as a place of worship. At first it seemed as if she simply knelt in prayer, but then she stood up and, as if following some unknown ritual, she began to disrobe. Within a few minutes she had let slip her clothes, removed her jewellery and unbound her tightly-plaited tresses. It was then that the horror began.

Suddenly, a low hiss broke from her lips and her skin began to peel, splitting from her forehead right down the length of her body and revealing the scaly, patterned flesh of a serpent. There was nothing human in this fiend and Gareth was horrorstruck at the sight of her.

As he heard more hissing sounds emanate from her, the serpent slithered entirely out of the human skin so that it lay lifeless on the floor, pale and ghastly in the cold moonlight that now illuminated the chamber with a watery glow. Then, just as strangely as the lady had shed her human form, the serpent now resumed the shape of the Lady of Lyonesse.

Gareth knew immediately there was some great wickedness in this castle that must be destroyed. This hideous creature, and doubtless many others of the same kind, must be put to the sword to destroy the evil. That night, as the castle slept, Gareth and the dwarf wreaked carnage, putting to death every living creature, including Linnet, which proved hard for Gareth to do. Yet when the blood from all those slain ran green and slimy and they reverted to their serpent form, Gareth knew that the deaths were justified. At first light he and the dwarf set the castle on fire, razing it to the ground so that nothing remained of it.

The ghastly evil at the castle was the doing of the enchantress Morgan le Fay, who was sworn to destroy the peace that Arthur had brought to the land by killing the bravest and noblest of the knights of the Round Table. However, Gareth's valiant action averted the doom she had prepared and he was determined that no one should know of her foul doings. He vowed that while he had breath in his body no natural or supernatural force would destroy the glory that rested with the knights of the Round Table.

While Gareth had been following his quest, his mother, Queen Margawse of Orkney, had arrived in Camelot to see how her youngest son fared and thus revealed his true identity. There were some red faces at court among those who had slighted Gareth when he had been only a kitchen boy. When Gareth returned shortly after this revelation, his brothers were overjoyed to see him and fiercely proud that he had turned out to be such a mettlesome knight.

The feast of Pentecost soon came round again and all the knights Gareth had conquered and their followers began to arrive at Camelot to swear allegiance. There was the Black Knight, who rode in a little sheepishly for he had no armour; there was the Green Knight, who made the court laugh and reminded some of Gawain's encounter with such a knight some Christmases past; then there came the rich Blue Knight, with 500 knights in his train; finally, there was the Red Knight, who proved himself to be most chivalrous now that he was freed of Morgan le Fay's foul enchantment.

It was a joyful time for Gareth – at last he was reunited with his family, and once again he met Katharine, the beautiful daughter of the Blue Knight who had travelled to court with her father. This time he knew that she was the maid he wished above all to marry, so the celebrations for his return concluded with the young couple's betrothal.

Sir Lancelot and the Lady Elaine

Sᴵʀ Lᴀɴᴄᴇʟᴏᴛ ᴡᴀs ᴛʜᴇ ʙʀᴀᴠᴇsᴛ and the most chivalrous of all King Arthur's knights; indeed, young and old alike thrilled to hear tell of his great exploits. Yet as reports of his glorious feats travelled far and wide, so did

rumours concerning his unlawful love for the queen, who was said to be as loving towards him in return. At first this gossip was deliberately spread by Mordred, the natural son of King Arthur and Morgan le Fay. When he was of an age to be made a knight, Mordred had been welcomed at court, despite the king's apprehension, for he had no other heir. However, this youth was a canker that burrowed deep to destroy the fair rose of chivalry that bloomed in Camelot. Eventually, the rumours about the love between Lancelot and Guinevere found common currency throughout the land and were widely held to be the truth.

Sir Lancelot had indeed loved the queen from the time he first saw her, as she had loved him too, yet there was never any impropriety in their behaviour towards each other. Indeed, Lancelot was constantly at pains to distract himself from his impossible and unlawful love by attaining ever greater feats of valour, even though he achieved these things to do honour to the queen. But if thinking thoughts of love constitutes guilt, then no two people were more guilty of loving each other than Lancelot and Guinevere.

The years passed and their unspoken passion grew rather than abated, becoming increasingly dangerous as there was no resolution for their emotions. Peace reigned throughout the land thanks to the strong and just rule of King Arthur and his knights of the Round Table, so now there was leisure for courtly pursuits and dalliances among the knights and ladies. Lancelot and Guinevere spent increasingly more time together, often meeting in the queen's secret garden where no prying eyes could oversee them. Yet Arthur took a simple delight that they should be so much together, for he thought it fitting that his beloved wife should be so close to his bravest knight and dearest friend.

One day a hermit came to Camelot and foretold how Sir Lancelot would one day have a son who would sit in the Siege Perilous, the seat of danger at the Round Table that only the purest knight ever born could occupy. When the queen heard these words she was consumed with jealousy; as she herself was barren and could never bear children, the prophecy could only mean that Lancelot would one day betray her with another woman.

Lancelot immediately guessed the queen's thoughts and knew that he should leave Camelot once more to spend his life as a knight errant, questing throughout the land and meeting whatever adventure came his way. The night before he left, he made his secret farewells to the queen in her walled garden where they sat close together in a secluded stone arbour, the evening air heavy with the scent of trailing columbine. A thoughtless nightingale serenaded the wretched lovers with its joyous notes. Breaking their unspoken pact never to touch, Lancelot held Guinevere in his arms, resting her head on his breast. She sobbed without cease as he stroked the soft, warm flesh of her neck, and he tried to soothe her with gentle words as he would a fretful horse.

'Will you love no one else but me?' begged Guinevere, at last able to speak through her tears.

'You know I can love no one else but you,' said Lancelot soothingly.

'Let me have something to remember you by,' said Guinevere. Thinking for a moment, Lancelot took an opal ring from the little finger of his left hand and placed it on the middle finger of Guinevere's left hand. However, the ring was too big, so Guinevere put it on a ribbon around her neck so that it would always be close to her heart.

Sir Lancelot left early next morning, watched by Arthur from high on the castle battlements. The king was filled with sadness to see this great knight depart, but only last night he had dreamt of Merlin's prophecy that his wife and his best friend would together betray him. He could never believe that the two people he held most dear would betray his trust, so he scornfully discounted all the rumours that continually reached his ears from throughout the kingdom.

It was many weeks since Sir Lancelot had ridden away, and so far he had met with no great adventure. He made a woebegone figure as he rode dejectedly through the land, for his heart was not on questing; all his waking and sleeping thoughts were of the queen from whom he had so recently parted.

His wanderings eventually led him close by the town of Corbin. As he rode across the bridge that led into this fair town, all the people dwelling there ran out into the streets, welcoming him and hailing him as the very flower of knighthood; and as he rode through their midst, they threw garlands of flowers around his neck and rose petals under the feet of his horse.

'Thank you for your kind welcome,' said Lancelot, feeling cheered for the first time since he had left Camelot. 'Tell me, citizens of Corbin, how may I serve you?' No sooner had he said these words than the people told him of the great danger that was in their town.

'There is a dolorous lady who for many years has been kept captive in our town's tower through witchcraft because an evil enchantress thought her too beautiful. We are constantly distressed by her piteous cries for she is held prisoner in a scalding bath. Indeed, our children stop up their ears for fear of hearing her screams.'

Sir Lancelot knew that he must rescue the poor maiden. 'Lead me to her,' he ordered, his own sad thoughts distracted by the prospect of this adventure.

'Take care, brave Sir Lancelot,' cried the townsfolk. 'Sir Gawain tried to rescue her and was scalded for his pains.'

However, Lancelot knew with a proud certainty that he would succeed where all others before him had failed. He was led without delay to the tower, where the townspeople left him, for they dared go no further. Once inside, he began to climb the stairway that led to the chamber in which the dolorous maiden was held. As he climbed up and up the stone steps, the air grew monstrously hot; steam hung in heavy clouds from ceiling to floor, making it difficult for Lancelot to catch his breath, and the slippery steps were treacherous underfoot, so his progress was slow.

Lancelot was determined to succeed in this quest, for it pained him to think of the beleaguered woman trapped for so long in this enchanted bath. When he reached the chamber door, which glowed white with a ferocious heat, he was forced to shield his eyes and face so they would not be burnt. As he paused to bless himself with the sign of the cross, the door miraculously swung open of its own accord and he entered the room. A billowing cloud of scalding steam engulfed him, but then it cleared slightly and across the chamber he could just discern a fire that burned continually, renewing itself through some witchcraft. Walking towards the tongues of red, flickering fire, he felt as hot as a boiled lobster inside his armour. His breathing came in laboured gasps but then, through the clearing steam, he saw the fairest woman he had ever beheld. As had been foretold, the best knight had finally come to rescue the dolorous lady.

Lancelot moved forward and plunged his arms into the bath, heedless of the scalding heat. Placing them underneath the maiden's shoulders and knees, he lifted her free from the cauldron in which she had been imprisoned and she was revealed as red and naked as a new-born babe.

This was the first time Lancelot had ever seen or touched a naked woman, and he was a little disturbed by the sight of such a beauteous one. Now he saw why she was called Elaine the Fair Lily, for she was tall and slender, and as unblemished as this fairest flower, even though the scalding water had blushed her silken skin to the dark ripeness of a red apple. Her gentle eyes gazed tenderly on her rescuer as he carried her downstairs and out of the tower. Amid much rejoicing, the ladies of the town came forward with blankets in which to wrap the damsel. Later, newly dried and clothed, she spoke to Lancelot.

'I am the daughter of King Pelles of the Wasteland Kingdom. I have been kept captive in this chamber for many years through the magic of Morgan le Fay. Let us go and give thanks to God for my safe deliverance.'

This done, they rode to the devastated kingdom of the maimed King Pelles so that he might meet his daughter's rescuer. When he learnt the name of this knight, he grew weak with excitement, for he knew a great prophecy was about to be fulfilled. That evening, when they sat down to supper in the ruined hall, there was no food set upon the table. Then, a white dove flew in through the highest window holding a little censer in her beak. As she passed over those assembled, the table was miraculously furnished with every manner of meat and drink. Moments later, an ethereal maiden, fair as an angel, passed through the hall carrying a golden vessel that resembled a chalice from ancient times. At the sight of this, the king and his companions fell to their knees in prayer. Lancelot simply watched with wonder at all these strange events.

'You have been blessed to see the Holy Grail pass. It is the most sacred relic in the whole world, for it is the chalice from which Christ drank at the Last Supper and it contains his blood that was spilt at his death.' As the king uttered these words, he seemed to gain in strength; the Grail had restored him and

given relief from the grievous wound in his side that refused to heal.

Lancelot gave thanks that he had been granted sight of this precious relic, for he had often heard that only the pure and good were worthy of the privilege. He had often thrilled to hear the legend of Joseph of Aramathea who had brought this sacred chalice to Britain from far across the sea.

As Lancelot sat wrapped in wonder, King Pelles watched him intently, his mind filled with the prophecy that Lancelot would beget a child on his daughter, the Fair Elaine, and that their child would be the knight who would heal King Pelles of the wound inflicted by Balin many years past. Once this ghastly wound was healed, his dead kingdom would be brought back to life. King Pelles pondered how this might be brought about, for everyone knew that Lancelot was a chaste knight who loved and served only Queen Guinevere.

Brisene, Elaine's lady-in-waiting, was a well-intentioned enchantress and she now approached King Pelles with a plan. Through her magic she could change Elaine's shape to that of the good knight's beloved Queen Guinevere, and to make the whole deception complete, she could even recreate the ring that Lancelot was known to have given her. The king agreed to this plan and that night one of his serving men went to Lancelot and gave him the counterfeit ring, telling him that the queen waited for him in the nearby Castle of Case. Lancelot was filled with wonder at the events taking place in this magical castle, but he did not think too deeply for he greatly wished to see the queen. If she had travelled to the wasteland kingdom to seek him out, there must be some danger to her. Without delay he called for his horse and rode through the still night to Case Castle. No guards or any of the entourage that Lancelot would have expected to accompany the queen were there, save for Brisene, who came out to greet him, saying that the queen had already retired.

'Can I bring you some refreshment?' asked Brisene. 'Or shall I lead you straight to your bedchamber? I will wake you early so that you can meet the queen first thing tomorrow.'

After his rapid night ride Lancelot wished for something to drink but the goblet that Brisene now offered him was laced with a magic potion that made his mind so befuddled that he was easily led to the bedchamber in which Elaine was waiting. Stripped naked by Brisene, he clambered into the bed but quivered with fright to find it already occupied. However, when he heard the queen's voice, his rapture knew no bounds, for at last it appeared she was willing to let him love her. Elaine was an eager participant in this deception, for she had loved this knight since her gaze first fell on him, and it filled her with pride that she would bear his child.

On that warm, dark night in the charmed bedchamber Lancelot made love to the woman he thought was the queen and she met his passion with equal rapture. There was no need for words to be spoken - all the language they needed was that of deep kisses and long, languorous caresses. When, at last, the lovers fell asleep, they lay entwined in each other's arms in a sleep too deep for dreams. And thus the prophecy came to be fulfilled, for that night Galahad was conceived.

Next morning, though the day was well begun, the chamber still remained in darkness, for Brisene had secured the doors and covered the window with heavy drapes so that not a chink of light might find its way in. It was her intention to lead Elaine from the chamber before the knight awoke so that Lancelot should not know how he had been deceived. However, Lancelot woke first and leapt from the bed to let in some light for he wanted to see the queen as she slept.

As the bright light streamed into the chamber, the startled knight saw not Guinevere but the sleeping Elaine, and the magic of the night faded. Despair overcame him as he saw how he had been deceived and Elaine was wakened by his groan. Rushing naked from the bed, she knelt at his feet begging for mercy, for she was certain he would kill her. Then she told him of the prophecy that had led to this deception, weeping bitterly to see the knight's distress.

Dressed only in his shirt and carrying his sword, Lancelot quitted the castle like a crazed man and wandered through the forest for many weeks, raging against the way he had been deceived. Eventually his scattered wits were restored and he returned to Camelot where he completely regained his health by close association with the queen. But his hunger for the queen was even more intense; he longed to be her lover now that he had tasted the delights of passion, but he made no mention of it and never told Guinevere of what had happened with Elaine at the Castle of Case.

Meanwhile, at Castle Carbonek, Elaine grew large with child and nine months after that enchanted night she gave birth to a boy whom she christened Galahad, his father's first name. She revelled in her babe's beauty and would allow no woman other than herself to suckle or care for him. She was determined to nurture this child herself, for the infant Galahad was her only reminder of the best knight in the world whom she loved with her whole being.

Some months after the birth of Galahad, Sir Lancelot's cousin, Sir Bors, was questing through the land when his travels brought him to Castle Carbonek. When he saw the infant Galahad and learnt of the child's parentage, he immediately took news of it back to Camelot. Here, it spread like wildfire and there was universal astonishment that Lancelot should have fathered a child on another woman when he was so devoted to Queen Guinevere.

The queen grew death-white when she heard of Galahad's birth, then she was consumed with anger, calling Sir Lancelot by every foul name she could think of. Her love for him was blemished by his public betrayal of her with the Lady Elaine.

It was not long after the birth of Galahad that King Arthur made ready to hold a great feast. He sent invitations far and wide throughout his kingdom, and when one reached Castle Carbonek, Elaine determined that she would go to Camelot for she longed to see Lancelot again. As befitted the daughter of a king, she arrived in great pomp, decked out in rich robes with a large retinue of knights and ladies, and she was counted one of the finest women at court. Although the king and his knights paid her great attention and many admiring glances were turned her way, her eyes sought only one man. But Sir Lancelot was too embarrassed and ashamed of what had taken place between them to talk to her, even though he still thought her the fairest woman he had seen.

Elaine was cut to the quick by Sir Lancelot's less than chivalrous behaviour. Where she had begun her journey confident that she would be reunited with her love, tears now fell without cease and she could not be consoled. Unable to endure her mistress's sorrow, Brisene again wove a spell so that Lancelot might once again sleep with Elaine.

Guinevere, however, was very suspicious of Elaine and had ordered that she sleep in a chamber near her own so that she could keep a close watch on any assignations. That night Brisene went to Lancelot's quarters and, using her skills of enchantment, took the hapless knight once more unwittingly to Elaine's bedchamber. Here, the couple immediately started to kiss and embrace, Lancelot all the while certain that he was with the queen.

Meanwhile, the queen had sent one of her ladies to Lancelot's chamber to make certain he was there. When this lady returned and reported that his bed was cold, the queen was frenzied with jealousy; she knew exactly where to find him, and later that very night her worst fears were confirmed. Sir Lancelot was wont to talk in his sleep about his love for the queen, and tonight, as sleep evaded Guinevere, she heard his voice muttering about his love for her. She turned livid with rage, for here was this seemingly faithful knight sleep-talking about his love for her while asleep in another woman's arms. Angered beyond endurance, Guinevere rose from her bed and paced around her

chamber; then, when her anger was spent, she started to wail in her wretchedness for the knight she thought had loved her but who was now entirely lost. As the sound of her weeping spread through the sleeping castle, it woke Sir Lancelot from his mumbling sleep in the chamber above. Hearing the queen's crying at such close quarters, he knew immediately that he had been deceived again. Turning to the woman who lay beside him, he saw with horror that it was the Lady Elaine.

At first he was numbed with shame, but then he was roused to anger. Dressed only in a nightshirt, he rushed towards the chamber window and fell from it, then ran like a wild man far away from the castle and into the sheltering forest. This time his wits seemed gone for good.

The next morning the disgraced Elaine was banished from court. Many knights were filled with sadness for they thought that Lancelot would never be seen alive again. But there were those, especially the evil Mordred's supporters, who took a perverted pleasure that Sir Lancelot had left the court in a state of madness. King Arthur had lost his most faithful supporter and his greatest knight, and the tired king was growing daily more vulnerable to the threat that his bastard son posed to his throne.

Guinevere's anger was soon spent and she sent Sir Bors and Sir Lionel to search for the demented Lancelot, for she already longed to see her good knight again. Surely he could not be far dressed only in his shirt? However, his cousins had to search for many months in their quest to find this sorely troubled knight.

During all this time Lancelot wandered cold, hungry and aimless, his wits scattered as if to the four winds, and fearful of any contact with his fellow man. Somehow he survived by drinking water from streams, eating berries from the forest and sometimes digging for roots in the ground. It was not long before his once powerful body was weakened, especially when he sustained injuries from encounters with wild beasts. As he wandered the land, his troubled mind saw strange creatures and these same beasts haunted his every footstep. In the trees and hills, beneath the streams and deep within the ground his visions called out to him and there was no place that Lancelot could find peace.

In time, his wanderings led him to the lands of King Pelles, where he was discovered sleeping in the gardens by servants. Although he was in rags and worn frail with hardship, his gentle chivalry touched them and they gave the poor derelict a fine red cloak. Once it had been placed around his shoulders, he looked so fine that they knew he must be some great person; only his eyes betrayed that he had fallen into madness. However, the good people of this land took him to the castle and cared for him. They put him to bed where he slept for many days and it was through the unselfish charity of these gentle people that Sir Lancelot gradually returned to sanity. Soon his body was whole again, but he could not remember who he was.

One balmy summer's evening, as he was walking in the castle garden, he sat on a stone bench to enjoy the early evening perfumes of the summer flowers and promptly fell asleep. It so happened the Lady Elaine was visiting the castle that day and had gone into the garden to look at the strange man whom the people had grown to love because he was so gentle and courteous. No sooner had the Lady Elaine looked upon this stranger than her heart seemed to stop beating and she fell down in a faint. The servants rushed to her aid and when her head had stopped its painful thudding she hardly knew what to do. Kneeling quietly beside Lancelot, she gazed upon the face which had altered so much since she had seen it last. Her eyes noted the scars and deeply etched wrinkles, and she gently removed the twigs and foliage that had found their way into his matted hair. Her eyes filled with tears as she tenderly examined his emaciated body that bore the marks of much hardship since he had fled from Camelot.

'How can I restore my love?' thought Elaine, and once more Brisene came to her mistress's aid. She wove a spell over Lancelot so that he would not wake for a day and a night and under this enchantment the sleeping knight was carried in a litter to the Castle of Carbonek where he was laid to rest in the chamber of the Holy Grail. So it was in this holy place that he woke to find his memory restored and his madness gone.

At first, Lancelot was both puzzled and agitated at his return to the Castle of Carbonek, and it was a further fourteen days before his agitation eased. Meanwhile, the gentle behaviour of Elaine touched him and made him feel whole, so he began to look with increasing tenderness on this lady. He begged her forgiveness for the hurt he had caused her and now asked her to be his love. Elaine was overjoyed and thought she would burst from happiness, for she and her little son were now to be reunited with his noble father.

King Pelles made them a gift of a castle which was situated off a distant coastline and Sir Lancelot ordered that it should be called Joyous Gard. Here, they lived in peace, but nothing Elaine could do would remove the sadness from Sir Lancelot's eyes, especially when he stood on the shoreline and turned his gaze in the direction of Camelot. His thoughts were always the same: of the king at whose side he no longer served, and of the queen whom he would love above all others until his dying breath.

When Lancelot's whereabouts became known, many knights came to visit him at Joyous Gard. They told him how he was still talked of at court and held

in high esteem, and Lancelot knew that he would one day return to Camelot. Indeed, before much more time had passed, he told Elaine of his intention, bringing the most piercing sorrow to her tender heart, for she knew that Lancelot would never return to her. However, before he departed she promised to send their son Galahad to Camelot when he was of an age to be knighted and he would receive this honour from his father's hand.

At first Queen Guinevere showed nothing but coldness towards Lancelot on his return. All at court could see how greatly he had aged and how he bore himself with an air of vulnerability which stood witness to the madness that had possessed him.

'His face is lined with the sorrows he has endured. He is no longer the young, chivalrous knight who rode out from this castle. How it breaks my heart to see him so,' thought the queen, who could no longer deny her feelings.

Thus, her coldness towards Lancelot thawed and the couple could hide their love no more.

What became of the Lady Elaine sorrowing at Joyous Gard? She pined now that her knight was gone and in her most despairing moments felt there was no meaning to her life. She grieved sorely at her loss, unable to eat or drink or find release in sleep. She withdrew from all around her, even the faithful Brisene, shutting herself in her bedchamber. Soon she was close to death in the bed that she had only so recently shared with Lancelot. Not even the sight of her beautiful little son could rouse her spirits.

Before long her beautiful body became pitifully thin and soon she was embracing death willingly. Her final instructions detailed how her son was to be cared for until he was old enough to be knighted. But her last wish was that Lancelot should see her wasted and lifeless body and feel some guilt for being the cause of her death.

Following Elaine's meticulous instructions, her servants carefully prepared their mistress for her last journey, dressing her hair and beautifying her now peaceful face so that she looked as radiant as she had ever been in life. They laced her into the gown that she had worn on her arrival at Camelot and placed the rings that Lancelot had given her on her stiff fingers. Thus decked out, she was laid in a barge that was to serve as her bier and surrounded with white lilies whose bright pollen spilt on to her robe making it appear that she shimmered in a golden light. Around her temples they placed a fragile crown of forget-me-nots and precious oils were sprinkled all over the boat's sad cargo. Black mourning drapes adorned with sweet-smelling flowers hung from the barge and trailed in the water. In Elaine's hand was placed a letter which said who she was and asked that King Arthur give her a Christian burial; it also requested that Sir Lancelot should keep vigil beside the bier the night before her burial.

Guided as if by some unseen power, this perfumed barge floated of its own accord from the fine castle of Joyous Gard to the river that flowed by Camelot. Here, it stuck fast by a stone bridge and many people came down to the riverbank to see the sight of the dead Lady Elaine. Eventually, the letter was taken from her hands and given to King Arthur who ensured that the lady's last wishes were completed as requested.

Lancelot, however, had no thoughts for the tragic Elaine, even though he was partly responsible for her death by causing her such despair. The knight who had once been the most chivalrous in the land was entirely besotted by the queen and held captive to her whims, so when she asked him not to keep the vigil as Elaine had sought, he readily complied. None the less, Guinevere remained jealous of Elaine, for she had given Lancelot the son who was destined to be the greatest knight that ever lived.

The Grail Quest

It was the eve of Pentecost and many knights of the Round Table had returned to Camelot to celebrate the great feast day. That evening a damsel rode into Camelot at great speed.

'Where is Sir Lancelot?' she called to those who were in the courtyard. When

he was pointed out to her, she went over to him. 'Ride with me, I beg you.'

'Why?' he asked, puzzled.

'There is something of great importance that you are destined to see tonight.'

Feeling that he could trust this damsel's words, Lancelot followed her on horseback. They cantered away from the castle and rode without pause through the forest until they came to a whitewashed abbey that was built in a clearing among the trees. The damsel led Lancelot into the abbey and to his amazement he was reunited with his cousins Bors and Lionel who had already been brought there. After the cousins had embraced each other in greeting, the damsel led Lancelot alone to another chamber and the abbess brought in the fairest and noblest young man he had ever seen.

'We have brought you here to see this youth whom we have been raising since he was of tender years,' said the abbess. 'We beg that you will knight him tomorrow at Camelot.'

'If it is this young man's wish, then I shall do so willingly,' said Lancelot.

The nuns then left Lancelot to talk with the youth, who impressed him greatly with his sense of chivalry and his gentle and courteous behaviour.

'Will you return to Camelot with my cousins and me tonight?' asked Lancelot.

'No,' replied the youth, 'but I shall come soon.'

When everything had been settled, the three knights returned to Camelot, riding through the night and escaping any unseen dangers in the forest. In fact, that night the moon shone so brightly that it seemed as if it were already daylight. The birds, too, were wakeful, singing and chirruping to each other as if aware that some great event was about to take place.

The knights reached Camelot as morning broke with its watery light. Without pausing to rest, they joined those who were already making their way to the church to celebrate the feast of Pentecost. When Mass was over, the congregation streamed out of the church into the bright, warm morning sunlight. Before breaking their fast, the knights made their way to the chamber of the Round Table and each took his denoted place. However, as they assembled they were met by an intriguing sight, for on the Siege Perilous – the seat of danger – they saw some words formed in letters of gold which read, 'He ought to sit here'.

Now it was well known that only the purest knight ever born could take his seat here with impunity; if an unworthy man should be foolhardy enough to sit upon the seat, the penalty was certain death.

'This year,' thought many knights, 'the seat will be filled.' Noticing the disquiet caused by the sight of these words, Arthur ordered that the seat be covered. A gleaming cloth of white samite was thrown over it, and this done the knights rose from the table to go and eat.

It was the custom that the feast at Pentecost should be preceded by some adventure, but as yet nothing had happened that could be counted as such. Suddenly, a squire rushed into the great hall.

'Come quickly, for I have seen a miraculous sight,' cried the squire breathlessly to the king.

'Catch your breath and then tell us exactly what you have seen,' said Arthur gently, hoping to calm the excited youth.

'There is a mighty red stone of marble floating in the river. What is even more wondrous, a richly jewelled sword with its pommel made of a single enormous ruby is embedded in the stone,' said the squire. 'It has become trapped against a reedy part of the bank and when I got closer to it, I could make out some words inscribed on the blade.'

'What does it say?' demanded Lancelot.

'It says, "For the best knight in all the world",' answered the squire.

'This sword is surely meant for you,' said Arthur, turning to Lancelot. 'You must be the one to draw it out of the stone.'

'It is not meant for me,' said Lancelot, for he knew within his heart that the adulterous desire he held for the queen made him no longer the purest knight. 'But I do believe this sword will mark the beginning of the quest of the Holy Grail.' He did not know from where this thought had suddenly occurred, but he was certain that his adventure the previous night presaged some great event.

Turning to his nephew Gawain, Arthur made the same suggestion, but he also refused to follow this adventure.

'Enough of this cowardly behaviour,' said Arthur angrily. 'Is there no one prepared to follow this adventure?'

'Believe me, I beg you, when I say that there are things at work here we are powerless to understand,' warned Sir Lancelot.

By now Arthur had lost all patience and he commanded all his knights to accompany him to the riverbank. Once there, many knights attempted to draw the sword from the stone but there was not one person who could accomplish this deed. Reluctantly, they repaired again to the Round Table where King Arthur decided that what they had witnessed today could be counted as an adventure, so they could now go and eat.

Just as they were about to leave the Round Table and return to the great hall, the doors of the chamber suddenly slammed shut of their own accord with a deafening crack. Fearing an attack, some knights immediately reached for their swords, then sheepishly remembered that no knight ever wore one at the Round Table. The gathering broke into a great uproar, when into its midst appeared an old hermit dressed entirely in white. Behind him stood a beautiful youth with a face of such translucent purity that everyone was silenced. He was dressed entirely in red, his burnished armour shining like garnets, and a cloak of similar hue was thrown around his broad shoulders. Lancelot saw it was the same young man whom he and his cousins had met the night before.

'I bring to you the last of Joseph of Aramathea's bloodline,' announced the hermit, Nacien. 'You have already witnessed great marvels today, but I tell you that adventures are at hand in distant lands which will far surpass anything you have yet seen.'

Without speaking further, he led the youth to the Siege Perilous and removed the gleaming cloth with a flourish. There, for all to see, were the golden letters, but this time they read, 'Galahad, the High Prince'.

'I bring you the knight who is destined to sit upon the seat of danger.' Nacien made to leave the chamber, but Galahad, the beautiful youth, detained him by taking his arm and spoke gently to the old man.

'Take my loving greetings with you to my beloved grandfather. Tell King Pelles that I shall soon return to heal him of his grievous wound and bring his wasteland kingdom back to life.'

Nacien bowed gravely at these words, then, leaning on his staff, he walked from the chamber, the sound of his steps fading into the distance. Indeed, as soon as he left the chamber, he disappeared from earthly sight forever, for he had completed the task that had been his destiny.

The knights who had been silent during these events now found their tongues and the chamber was filled with a rising hum of chatter. Some knights had also realized that Galahad was none other than Lancelot's son by the fair Elaine. The suspense of all that had passed was now relieved, so with appetites sharpened, they repaired to the great hall to eat. When the feast was over, King Arthur took Galahad down to the river to see the sword that was embedded in the red marble stone.

'This is my sword,' exclaimed Galahad. 'See, I carry its scabbard. Nacien told me that I should find this very sword – the sword with which Balin slayed his beloved brother Balan. This is the weapon with which he wounded my grandfather with the dolorous stroke, causing his kingdom to be turned into a wasteland.' With these words Galahad bent down, clasped both hands around the hilt and effortlessly drew the sword from the stone. The knights of the Round Table simply looked on in wonder.

Shortly after these marvels, a damsel, fair as an angel, rode out of the forest and into the castle, where she was immediately conducted to the king.

'I bring you great tidings, for the Holy Grail will be seen at Camelot this very day,' she said.

At her words King Arthur felt joy mingled with sorrow, for he remember- ed that Merlin had prophesized the start of the quest for the Holy Grail as the last time all the knights of the Round Table would be as one illustrious band.

Later that day Lancelot was reunited with Galahad, his only son whom he had not seen since leaving him as a child at Joyous Gard. He was filled with awe in his son's presence for Galahad had a majesty that defied his tender years. Moreover, he did not judge his father harshly for the unkind treatment he had meted out to his mother. In accordance with Elaine's final wishes, Lancelot then knighted their son.

Away from the watchful eyes of the court, father and son talked for many satisfying hours and Sir Lancelot was not ashamed to shed many tears of happiness. He saw beyond all doubt that his peerless son would accomplish all that he himself had failed to do. And when, at last, they returned to the teeming court, the king and the queen made much of Galahad, although it was not without a pang that Guinevere looked upon the youth who was the son she could never have. However, Galahad showed her such courtesy and honour that she loved him well and all her jealous feelings fell away.

As word of all these wonders spread rapidly throughout the countryside, those who dwelt within half a day's distance of the castle made their way with all speed to Camelot. From the oldest to the youngest, by cart, horse or foot, the roads were awash with travellers. No person who drew breath was ready to pass up being witness to the most miraculous day in their lives.

After evensong, when the knights were once more seated at the Round Table, there came a mighty crack of thunder that seemed to make the earth quake. Then, a roaring wind swept through the castle, causing the wooden doors to slam shut and the candles and reed lamps to flicker. All the knights, except Sir Galahad, sprang to their feet. The next instant the chamber was filled with a beam of light seven times brighter than the brightest summer sunlight. Every knight was bathed in this light and when each looked upon his neighbour, he thought him fairer than ever before; indeed, everyone in the castle that night felt as if he or she had been filled with a wondrous grace.

Not a sound was heard in the chamber, until a snow-white dove flew in by an upper window and hovered above the awestruck knights, filling the air with perfume from a tiny censer she held in her beak. A moment later the Holy Grail entered, gleaming beneath a veil that hid the sacred vessel from men's sinful eyes.

As the Sangrail remained high above the seated knights suspended on the beam of light, each man felt as if he had found paradise, for all spiritual and temporal hunger was satisfied at the moment of the Holy Grail's passing. The Sangrail disappeared as quickly as it had come and all those present remained rapt in wonder at what it had been their privilege to see.

'Praise be to God for what we have seen,' cried Sir Gawain leaping to his feet. 'I vow I shall not rest or partake of wordly pleasures until I have seen the Grail again without its veil.'

As though floodgates had been opened, every knight now rose and vowed that he would not rest until he had followed and succeeded in this quest. With one voice the knights determined to depart the next morning on the greatest quest the world had ever seen.

'I cannot deny you this adventure, my faithful knights,' said Arthur. 'Let this quest last for a year and a day.' So great was his emotion that he could speak no further when asked for his blessing. He wept at all that passed, for it was as Merlin had foretold: tomorrow his glorious knights would leave to follow the quest of the Holy Grail. As Arthur looked around at these men he knew so well, whose faces bore witness to the strength of their resolve, he knew that he would never again see these brave knights all together.

The night was spent in feverish preparation for departure the next morning, but great sadness permeated the feverish labours and there were many tears among the women who loved these knights and wished they might travel with them. Through the night, men and women, whether old or young, high or low-born, rich or poor, all were united in their desire to see everything ready for the knights' departure.

Galahad rested in King Arthur's own bed that night as the king sought no repose; he was too full of sorrow as he watched his knights make ready for their great adventure. When first light broke, streaking the still grey sky with pink fingers of sunlight, the knights dressed in their newly burnished armour and went to the church to hear Mass. When the service and blessing were over,

Arthur counted how many knights would follow the quest – 150, the full complement of the Round Table.

Without further delay the knights mounted their horses, which pawed the ground, snorting and tossing their heads, anxious to be galloping over the open countryside. From the steps that led up to the great hall Arthur surveyed his knights for the last time. Calling out his blessing for good fortune and a safe conclusion to their quest, he signalled for the castle gates to be thrown open and raised his hand in a final gesture of farewell.

Without a backward glance, the knights rode away from Camelot, their harnesses jangling and the ground vibrating with the weight of their horses' hooves. As they streamed down the hill from Camelot, they looked like a flowing ribbon of colour; their armour glinted bright in the sunshine and the pennants on their newly-sharpened lances fluttered with the bright designs of the knights' devices. At the head of the 'ribbon' Galahad rode alongside his father to inspire their companions on this quest.

The first day the knights rode in a single body, resting through the warm night beneath the twinkling stars. On the second day the knights split into smaller groups, riding out in different directions to face whatever adventures might come their way.

Sir Galahad, however, rode alone. He met with no adventure for four days until he came to a whitewashed abbey nestled deep within a forest. Here he was welcomed by the monks and led to the guest chamber where he found two other knights, Sir Bagdemagus and Sir Uwan.

'We made our way to this place because we heard tell on our travels that a miraculous shield rests in the chapel, which only the best knight in the world may carry,' said Sir Bagdemagus.

'But,' added Sir Uwan, 'if an unworthy knight takes the shield, he will meet with disaster within three days. In that case it will be returned to the chapel until the best knight comes to claim it.'

The three knights then went to the chapel to see this marvellous object. The shield, which was made of pure white cloth stretched over a wooden frame, had a red cross marked on it.

'Sir Galahad,' said Bagdemagus, 'I know I am not the most worthy knight but I wish to follow this adventure. I ask that you remain here for three days and if I should fail in this quest and the shield is returned here, I can think of no worthier knight than you to follow this adventure.'

Galahad agreed, so Bagdemagus and his squire set off with the shield. They had gone but a short way from the abbey when they came to a pleasant valley in which another abbey nestled. Suddenly, a knight dressed in dazzling white armour and carrying a white spear from which fluttered a white cloth of gleaming samite, galloped out of the abbey. Without issuing a challenge, he rode at great speed towards Bagdemagus and struck him such a blow that it pierced his breastplate, went straight through his chainmail vest and badly wounded Bagdemagus in the side.

'It was a great folly to take that shield,' said the White Knight, 'for you are not worthy of it.' With these words he dismounted and took back the shield from where it lay beside the fallen knight. Turning to Bagdemagus's squire, he said, 'Take him back gently to the abbey and give this shield to Sir Galahad. Tell him he is the only knight worthy to bear it on his arm.'

The squire, who was named Melias, did as he was instructed. With great care he carried Bagdemagus back to the abbey, where he was taken to the chapel and laid in front of the altar for his wound to be tended. When Melias told Galahad what the mysterious knight had said, Galahad and the squire rode out to meet him. It was not long before they came to the valley, and as before the White Knight appeared, his white armour gleaming so brightly that Galahad and Melias had to turn their eyes away. He greeted Galahad with great courtesy and told him the story attached to the shield.

'After Joseph of Aramathea had taken Christ down from the cross at Calvary, he journeyed to the city of Sarras where King Evelake ruled. This king had been waging war against the Saracens and Joseph told him that he would certainly be slain in the forthcoming battle if he did not become a

Christian. The king did not take much persuading, so he was soon baptized. Joseph then made the king a shield with his own hands, stretching white cloth over a wooden frame, and telling Evelake that it would protect him in battle. It proved to be a most miraculous shield, for one man whose hand was severed in the thick of fighting was healed the moment he touched it. Indeed, no man feared death in Evelake's army while the king carried this shield, and it was not long before the Saracens were defeated. Joseph and Evelake then embarked on many travels which, in time, led them to the land of Britain.

'Before they had passed many years in this land, Joseph grew sick and was soon on his deathbed. Evelake remained at his side all the while and when the end drew close, he asked for some token by which he might remember the holy man. At this, Joseph asked for the shield to be brought to him. Now, part of Joseph's infirmity was that he had a nosebleed that could not be staunched, so he marked a sign of the cross in his own blood on the shield so that Evelake should always remember him whenever he looked upon it. Joseph also told Evelake that no one could bear this shield with impunity until Galahad, the good knight destined to carry it, was born. Finally, Joseph told of the many marvellous deeds that Galahad would achieve, the first of which would occur fifteen days after he had received his knighthood.'

As the White Knight finished speaking, Galahad realized that exactly fifteen days had elapsed since he was dubbed. Melias, who was the son of the King of Denmark, heard these words and begged Sir Galahad to dub him a knight, which he duly did.

Next morning the newly dubbed Sir Melias asked to ride with Sir Galahad on the Grail Quest, so the two knights journeyed together. For two days they trekked through the forest until they came to a place where the path divided. As they deliberated which path to follow, a man appeared from out of the trees.

'Good sirs, you must each choose a way forward,' he said. 'A good and worthy knight may pass unscathed through the right path. The left path leaves all but the best knight in the world open to attack.' After giving this warning, the man disappeared before they could question him further.

'Let my first quest be to take the left path,' implored the impetuous Sir Melias who was anxious to prove his knightly mettle. 'I am ready to face whatever danger comes my way.'

Galahad agreed to this request and, without delay, Melias rode down the left path and soon disappeared into the dense forest. He rode for two days but met with no adventure until he saw that the forest was petering out. Soon he found himself in a fertile meadow where the green grass was mingled with the fresh colours of daisies and buttercups. At the far corner of the meadow he

thought he saw an imposing throne, but on closer inspection he saw it was the stump of a tree that grew, or had been carved, so wondrously that it could have been fashioned out of gold with all the wood's knots and grain forming an intricate pattern. On the seat of this wooden 'throne' was set a fine golden crown which gleamed in the bright daylight.

As he rode closer, Melias noticed a most welcome sight, for there on the ground, close by the throne, was a silken cloth on which were laid many dishes of fine food with flagons of wine. Being young and impetuous, Melias acted before truly considering the consequences of his actions. He sat down on the ground and started to eat and drink, then picked the crown from the seat and playfully placed it on his head. He then sat down on the wooden throne careless of whether he did right or wrong. No sooner had he done so than a knight mounted on a powerful warhorse crashed out of the nearby trees.

'Defend yourself, for you have taken what is not yours,' bellowed the knight as he charged at full tilt towards Melias.

'Sweet heavens help me,' prayed Melias, lifting his eyes skywards as he flew to mount his horse. No sooner was he in the saddle than the knight was upon him, attacking him with a wild ferocity and piling blow upon blow. Melias fought vigorously, but when he received a grievous blow to his right side, he fell to the ground almost dead.

Meanwhile, Galahad's journey down the right path had brought him to this very place, and when he saw his erstwhile companion lying sorely wounded and helpless in the meadow, he rode over to see what had occurred.

'Who did this to you?' Galahad asked Melias, greatly distressed to see how this young knight had been treated. Melias could scarcely reply.

'Help me,' he whispered, 'help me for I must confess my sins before I die.'

Galahad dismounted and went over to comfort the gravely wounded knight. As he cradled him in his arms, unlacing his armour to ease the pressure on his wound, he looked towards the trees and caught sight of Melias's attacker who was skulking in the shadows of the nearby forest.

'Coward!' shouted Galahad. 'Fight me at your peril, for I shall avenge the way you attacked my fellow knight.'

At these words the knight spurred his horse forward, so Galahad laid Melias gently on the ground and leapt into his saddle, riding at speed towards his adversary. Their lances cracked together but Galahad's struck home, piercing the other knight's shoulder and passing straight through his body. With a startled gasp of pain his opponent fell to the ground. Galahad swiftly dismounted and drew his sword, cutting at the befuddled knight with merciless strokes until he finally slashed his arm off. The maimed knight tried to flee and Galahad, who judged there was no further danger of attack, returned to the fast-fading Melias who was almost dead. Lifting him gently on to his horse, he took him back to the abbey where a monk cared for his wounds. Miraculously, within three days, Melias was fully restored to health and ready to resume his quest.

As he had tended Melias, the monk explained that he had been gravely wounded because he had carried pride in his heart. When he had taken the

golden crown, he had shown covetousness. He had been overthrown by the two deadly sins of pride and theft.

The monk gave Galahad his blessing and the good knight set off once more on his quest. This time he rode alone, meeting with many adventures and accomplishing many brave deeds. Throughout the land his fellow knights who followed the quest of the Holy Grail were in wonder at the tales of chivalry and bravery they heard about the knight in red armour who carried a white shield marked with a red cross, for they did not know it was Sir Galahad.

The Grail adventure now rests with Sir Perceval, son of the mighty King Pellinore. He had first arrived at court as a simple country boy but went on to win great glory for his simple knightly virtues of truth and honour.

Perceval rode for many weeks in quest of the Holy Grail but met with no great adventures. Far and wide on his travels he heard tell of the glorious exploits of a knight in red armour who carried a white shield with a red cross. Then, one day, he met an old hermit who told him that this would be the knight to succeed in the Grail Quest.

The hermit also told him that the knight would far surpass his father in strength and glory. When Perceval heard these words he knew the knight to be Galahad and realized that he would be his guide rather than his adversary on this quest.

Finally, this hermit told Perceval to make his way with all speed to Castle Carbonek where the maimed King Pelles would be found, for there he would see great wonders.

On and on Perceval rode, until some days later he arrived at a well-fortified house. As night was fast approaching, he asked for shelter and was well looked after. The next morning he continued on his quest, passing by a monastery where he stopped to pray. As he was kneeling, the strangest sight he had ever seen entered the chapel. A coffin covered with a cloth was carried in by four young squires and placed before the altar. Suddenly, Perceval heard a faint voice calling for help and realized that this frail sound emanated from inside the coffin. Approaching it, he drew back the cloth and saw an ancient man wearing a crown. He was wondrously wizened and appeared to have lived at least 100 years. He lay naked to the waist and these exposed areas of his body were sorely wounded with sword cuts.

'Who is this man?' asked Perceval to a monk close by.

'He is King Evelake,' said the monk. 'He first came into this land with Joseph of Aramathea when the Holy Grail was seen openly throughout this land. These holy men were nourished daily by the Grail's power until, one day, Evelake looked too closely upon its majesty. God was much displeased at this action and struck him almost blind for seeing what he should not have seen. Evelake then prayed that he might not die until he had seen the knight who would succeed in the Grail Quest. At this a mighty voice answered from the heavens that he should remain alive until that time had come. Moreover, when this knight comes he will heal Evelake's wounds with a kiss and restore his sight, also freeing him from the prison of his mortal body. Evelake has waited 300 years for this knight, and through all that time he has been kept alive through the miraculous power of the Holy Grail, for he has not once eaten or drunk of mortal food.'

'How came he by these terrible wounds?' asked Perceval, for they looked so severe that they would kill most men.

'He received them fighting against the heathen Saracens before he came into this land,' said the monk. 'But tell me, good knight, are you of the Round Table?'

'I am Perceval de Galles, knight of the Round Table,' replied Perceval.

'God be praised,' said the monk, 'for now the quest for the Holy Grail must be abroad and the knight for whom King Evelake awaits will soon come and heal his wounds so he may die in peace.' When he carried this news to King Evelake, the old man was filled with joy and tears rolled down his ravaged face.

Perceval left the monastery to continue on his quest, searching through many places for where he might find the Red Knight with the white shield who would lead him to the Holy Grail. One day on his travels he was set upon by twenty knights who would have killed him had not that very knight come to his aid. When he had freed Perceval from danger, he galloped off at speed before Perceval had opportunity to thank him. He would have ridden after him had

not his horse been slain by the knights who had attacked him. As Perceval stood in this forsaken place, at a loss as to where he would find another horse, he saw a yeoman riding by on an exceedingly ugly and clumsy farmhorse.

'Good day, good yeoman. I need a horse to continue my quest. I beg you let me buy yours. Here, take this golden ring in payment,' said Perceval.

'If you want my horse, you will only get it by force,' snarled the bad-tempered yeoman.

Perceval was greatly irritated to meet with this response for he was now left in an ignominious situation. By now, night had fallen and there was nothing further that he could do that day, so he unbuckled his armour and lay down on the ground to sleep. However, after only a few hours, Perceval awoke with a start at the sound of a woman whispering in his ear.

'Grant me a wish when I ask it of you,' she said, her warm breath filling Perceval's ear. 'If you agree to this, then I will bring you a fine horse.'

Now wide awake, Perceval agreed with alacrity and the woman slipped away, returning shortly with the finest black stallion decked out in a magnificent harness that Perceval had ever seen. He mounted this powerful horse, which wheeled round energetically, for it was in sore need of some hard riding to calm it.

The horse had a fierce will of its own and Perceval found it difficult to handle as it careered off into the dark night. On and on the beast raced without cease, as if pursued at close quarters by some fiend. In the darkness Perceval could hear the sound of a rushing torrent which, from its increasingly loud roar, seemed to be drawing closer and closer. He could not see anything as he peered into the darkness around him, for the night was pitch black with no moon or stars to throw light on where this creature led him. Perceval began to feel afraid.

Putting all his trust in God, he quickly made a sign of the cross. At this the black stallion shied and tossed Perceval from his back, filling the night air with a horrible neighing. Then, with a single leap, the horse jumped into the torrent below. At once Perceval knew the stallion had been a fiend and he gave thanks to God for his safekeeping. He remained in prayer for the rest of the night that he might be kept safe from all such dangers.

When rosy-fingered dawn first lit the sky he saw to what place the fiend had led him. He was high on a wild mountain top which, as far as the eye could see, was totally surrounded by water. Wild beasts roamed through the region below but he could see no sign of other men. As he climbed down the mountain, he came upon a young lion fighting with a young serpent, each testing their skill and strength. Then, a great lion appeared out of the shrubland, roaring as if he possessed all he surveyed. Slithering behind this beast was a giant serpent, and soon these two creatures began to fight. Perceval watched mesmerized as the serpent coiled around the lion's torso with deathly caresses, spitting venom from its poisoned, forked tongue.

Perceval was filled with foreboding that the lion who fought with such daring nobility should be destroyed. Drawing his sword, he rushed towards the creatures and slashed at the serpent, severing its body into three large pieces. For this great gesture the lion was now Perceval's friend and would not leave his side, rubbing against him with his great shaggy head, pawing the ground and fawning on him like a lap dog. At night Perceval slept snuggled against the lion for warmth, and during the day he travelled in safety through this land that was filled with many strange and savage creatures.

One night, Perceval had a most perturbing dream in which he saw two ladies - one seated on his companion, the lion, and the other riding on the serpent he had slain. These slender damsels told him that the following morning he would meet the sternest test to his knighthood, for he was destined to meet with the most powerful dragon in all the world. When he awoke Perceval was greatly disquieted, and it was in low spirits that he came upon a priest - the first human being he had seen for many days. The priest had sailed to this land in a little coracle, for he had some great news to impart.

'Will I ever escape from this wild place?' asked Perceval despairingly. 'Will I ever follow the Grail Quest again?'

'My son, by remaining a good and true knight you will succeed in all your heart's desires, for while you remain so, no man or fiend can harm you,' said the priest.

Then Perceval told the priest of his dream. 'Who is it I shall fight?' he asked.

'I cannot tell you, but remember, you will be victor in this struggle although you will first be shamed,' answered the priest.

That day Perceval sat with the lion by the water's edge looking out over the glassy green sea that surrounded the land. Suddenly, he thought he saw the faint outline of a ship on the horizon; as it drew nearer, he saw his eyes had not deceived him. When it was close to land, he saw that the ship was entirely storm-torn with its black sails hanging in tatters and everything on deck blackened as if burnt by lightning. His eye then lit upon a lovely woman dressed in ragged black robes who clung to the broken masthead in dire despair as the ship was driven on to the rocks that hugged the shoreline.

'Perceval, Perceval!' she cried wretchedly, somehow knowing the knight's name. 'Help me! Help me and I will tell you where to find the mighty Red

Knight with the white shield whom you seek. I have seen him pursuing some churlish fellows in the forest that lies on the other side of this place.' She spoke in such dulcet tones that Perceval was quite captivated.

'Madam, I will help you most willingly,' he replied, and without further ado he clambered down to the rocky shore. There, using all his strength, he pushed the ship free of the rocks so that it floated once more on the clear, deep water. He then manoeuvred the boat to a place on the shore where the lady

could land without any great difficulty. When she alighted, he saw that she
was ten times fairer than he had first thought.

'Good Perceval, you have saved my life and I will always be in your debt.
But let me ask a further boon of you. There is a knight who has siezed my lands
and my castle. I beg you to fight as my champion and I will reward you with all
that I possess,' said the lady, mesmerizing Perceval with her limpid eyes.

171

'Of course I will fight for you,' said Perceval staunchly, so they set out on this quest. However, as they walked through the land surrounded by water, the lady suddenly changed her tune and began to tell Perceval many tales of the Red Knight's wickedness. She had such a winning way about her that Perceval soon believed all she said was true.

'Beware, too, Perceval of the man you thought to be a priest – he is a nimble-witted enchanter who wishes to lead you astray,' warned the lady.

The day now grew hot and sultry, and a heat haze hung over the land. After his disturbed sleep last night, Perceval felt increasingly fatigued so he lay down to rest for a short while.

Soon he fell fast asleep, watched closely by the lady who sat down beside him. When he woke, the lady handed him a brimming cup of warm red wine which he gulped willingly, for he had not tasted good wine since starting on this quest. Shortly afterwards he began to experience the most tender feelings towards the lady beside him.

'Lady, let me kiss you,' said the enamoured Perceval.

'Kiss me, then,' she replied. And so he did for the first time in his life.

'Let me love you,' begged the amorous Perceval eventually, no longer satisfied by mere kisses and made bold by the lady's willing compliance. She smiled sweetly as if well pleased by his entreaties.

'I will not let you love me unless you promise to do whatever I command,' said the lady, confident in her power over the enchanted knight.

As chance would have it, they saw a fine pavilion pitched nearby that seemed to have appeared as if by magic. The lady led Perceval inside and they found a bed made up with cool silk sheets and soft, goose-feather pillows in soothing green colours. To Perceval's astonishment the lady started to disrobe with a distinct lack of modesty; soon she was stark naked, whereupon she lay gracefully on the bed. The sight of this beautiful woman was more than the chaste Perceval could bear. Filled with lust, he tore off his clothes and in a very short time was lying down, equally naked, beside her.

Just as Perceval was about to take possession of this beauteous woman, enfolding her in a passionate embrace prior to lovemaking, his eye caught sight of the cruciform made by the hilt of his sword. In an instant he perceived the mortal danger he was in; he grasped the sword, holding its hilt before him and it was as if he had been suddenly turned to stone. The woman now lay on the bed panting and heaving with a vile hissing rage. Suddenly, the pavilion disintegrated about them, scattered asunder by a great roaring wind; then, it was sucked up into the air and transformed into furling ribbons of black smoke. With an awful, blood-curdling scream, the woman rose high into the sky where she was changed into a black, ravening bird. This creature's beak was pulled back in ferocious anger as it hovered over the cowering Perceval and he feared the fiend would swoop down to pluck out his eyes in vengeance for resisting a fatal temptation. But then, flapping her large black wings so the air was filled with a dreadful racket, the bird flew up high into the sky and was soon lost to Perceval's sight.

The poor knight was distraught that he could have been so easily deceived by a fiend, and grief-stricken at his own frailty. Only a chaste knight, who had never known a woman, could succeed in the Grail Quest, and he had so nearly surrendered his virginity. His hands bled profusely as he clasped the sword's blade, and in distress he plunged it straight into his body. However, some guarding spirit was keeping watch over Perceval, for although the wretched knight had meant to pierce his heart, the blade somehow slipped and pierced his thigh instead.

The selfsame priest with whom Perceval had spoken earlier that day now reappeared. He comforted Perceval and told the sorrowing knight what all these events had meant.

'Take heart, good Perceval, counselled the priest. You were tempted but have resisted the greatest evil in all the world. In the end you overcame the seducive blandishments of the most powerful fallen angel, Lucifer, the devil himself.'

Many knights who had embarked on the quest for the Holy Grail were already becoming weary of this adventure because they knew they would never succeed. It had been foretold that, of all the knights who sought the Grail, only three would triumph. Sir Gawain and many others had grown weary of their adventures, so they turned their horses once more towards Arthur's kingdom

and made their way back to
Camelot. Sir Lancelot, however,
continued on the Grail Quest, for he knew
beyond doubt that the mighty Red Knight with the
white shield was his son, Galahad, who had already
won great glory in this adventure. He longed above all else
to ride with him on this, the greatest adventure known to men.

The story now leaves Sir Perceval and rests with the adventures of Sir Bors.
His journey took him to many lands, until one day he rode through a strange,
dark forest where he came upon a tall and lifeless tree amid the flourishing
greenness. Nesting high in its topmost branches was the strangest creature

Bors had ever seen, for it was half raven and half swan. That night, as he slept on the forest floor, Sir Bors dreamt of this black and white creature and it seemed to speak to him, offering him all the riches in the world if he would do its bidding. When Bors awoke, so vivid was this dream that he remembered it entirely and he was greatly puzzled as to what it meant.

As he rode on through the forest, he saw that the path divided into two overgrown tracks. Riding closer, he was appalled to see two knights mounted on horseback thrashing a defenceless man whom they were dragging along the ground between their horses. The poor wretch's naked body was covered with angry weals, and so great was his distress, that he could barely cry out.

Without hesitation Bors rode up to intervene and then saw to his horror that the beaten man was his brother Lionel whose body was cut by more than 100 strokes. The attackers immediately dropped the ropes and galloped off like scalded cats. Bors rushed to where his wounded brother lay when, from the other forest path, he heard the piteous crying of a woman's voice. Moments later a powerfully armoured knight rode out of the forest with a tiny maiden slung across the front of his saddle, her nut-brown hair hanging down and almost trampled by the horse's hooves.

'Help me, good sir! Help me to escape from this brutish knight who wishes to dishonour me,' cried the maiden.

What was Bors to do? Both his brother and this damsel were in sore need of his protection. God keep my brother safe until I may speedily return to him, prayed Bors silently and raising his eyes to heaven. Then, having made his choice, he set off in pursuit of the knight who had abducted the maiden.

'Release this lady,' he cried when he had caught up with the abductor. The knight stopped and looked scornfully at Bors, then putting the maiden down from his horse, he turned to fight. Bors, however, was ready to meet his attack and swiftly killed him with a blow that pierced the breastplate.

'How can I thank you, good knight, for you have surely saved my life? Please, I beg you, come to my castle nearby so I can give you proper thanks,' said the maiden gratefully.

Although Bors was greatly concerned for his injured brother, he decided to accompany the maiden back to the castle where he was warmly welcomed and a lavish feast prepared in his honour. Bors grew increasingly anxious to be gone but his hosts insisted he should stay, and he knew they would think him discourteous if he left without taking any of the refreshment prepared for him. However, he had vowed to eat only bread and water on the quest for the Holy Grail, so he would not even taste the delicious morsels and piquant sauces with which the damsel tried to tempt him.

At the first opportunity Bors left the castle, returning to the spot where he had last seen his brother, but to his horror he was no longer there. He searched all around with increasing panic but eventually returned despondently to the damsel's castle and asked to shelter for the night. His body was much fatigued, but his mind would not give him rest, as he tossed and turned throughout the night, grieving for his brother.

In the early hours of the morning, the little damsel slipped into Bors's

bedchamber and used many seductive wiles to tempt him into loving her; but the knight would not succumb, no matter how much she flirted and pouted in her attempts at seduction. For over an hour she continued with her winsome ways, fluttering her thick, dark lashes over her limpid grey eyes until finally she stamped her foot in irritation.

'So be it, sir knight. If you will not love me then I shall order twelve of my waiting ladies to be thrown from the topmost tower of my castle,' she cried vindictively. Soon the top tower was filled with twelve wailing maidens who pleaded with Bors to spare them by sleeping with their mistress.

'Do you really wish to be the cause of these maidens' deaths? Surely it is less of a crime to love me than to allow these innocent women to die,' said the lady of the castle.

Although heavy of heart, Bors would not yield. He cried out for all the heavenly powers to protect him and made the sign of the cross to firm his resolve. No sooner had his hand touched his breast to complete this benediction than a mighty wind blew up and roared through the castle, catching up the women and whirling them into the sky. Suddenly, their womanly form disintegrated and they were transformed into screaming streaks of black matter, which fell to the earth in a shower of black soot. Thus, Bors's strong resolve had saved him from foul fiends in womanly form.

Making his way rapidly from the castle, he had not ridden far before he met with a hermit who told him that the bird he had seen the day before represented the struggle of good against evil from which he had just emerged victorious. But all Bors's thoughts were now with his brother; he knew that he had erred in not saving the sorely wounded Lionel and wondered if he were still alive.

He wandered through the countryside in great dejection until he came to a fine tower that was built on top of a steep hill that was surrounded by pleasant and fertile pastures. He rode towards this place and soon met with a squire who told him of a great tournament that was to be held there the very next day. Bors greatly wished to meet with some of his fellow knights who followed the Grail Quest as they might have news of his brother. As he rode towards the tower, he spied a knight on the path ahead of him; drawing closer, he saw to his great joy that it was his brother Lionel whom he had feared dead.

'Brother, I thought you had been killed. You live, sweet heavens, you live,' cried an incredulous Bors.

'And what of it, you worthless dog,' spat out Lionel. 'If I am alive, it is not of your doing.' Bors tried to make his brother see reason, but Lionel's anger was very great.

'If you had been in that situation, I would have gladly laid down my life for you,' cried an aggrieved Lionel, and flew at Bors with his sword drawn. 'I will kill you for your betrayal.' In a frenzy, he hacked and slashed at Bors who was soon rendered helpless.

'Mercy,' cried Bors, but Lionel ignored his pleas; it seemed as if he were possessed by some demon. When all seemed lost, Bors heard a mighty rumbling voice from the heavens.

'Brothers, do not kill each other, for if you do, you shall forfeit your eternal souls.' As this awesome voice was heard, a cloud of crackling blue flame came between the two brothers and so great was its heat that both men were forced to raise their shields for protection. However, both shields were burned to a cinder and the brothers fell to the ground in a swoon.

When at last Bors stirred, he heard the same voice crack through the sky like thunder and this time it explained that Lionel had been possessed by a demon who had wished to destroy Bors for failing to succumb to all the temptations that had been put in his way on this quest.

The same voice now told Bors to mount his horse and ride to a ship that he would find at anchor on the nearby shore. On reaching this ship he found Perceval waiting for him and these two good knights, who had succeeded through so many adventures, were joyfully reunited. Both knew that they only lacked Sir Galahad, the Red Knight with the white shield, for once he arrived they could continue on the final adventure of the Quest of the Holy Grail.

Sir Galahad continued his travels through many lands, having become known as the High Prince for the great deeds he had accomplished. As he rested one night in the open, a maiden came to him and bade him to follow her to a ship that was moored nearby.

'Sir Bors and Sir Perceval are waiting for you on the enchanted ship. Hurry, for it is waiting to take you to the Holy Grail - it cannot set sail unless you are aboard.'

Asking no questions, Galahad rode with the maiden to a small creek where the ship lay at anchor. This mysterious boat was hung with shining sails of samite that glistened in the moonlight. No sooner was Galahad aboard than the ship moved off on its own accord, sailing gently though there was no crew to man it. The ship obviously knew its course; it soon passed beyond the shelter of the creek and forged ahead on the night swell into the open sea.

The three knights were well pleased to be reunited and embraced each other warmly, for they knew the Quest for the Holy Grail would soon be completed. The maiden stayed on board with the knights and showed them the many wonders that were to be seen on the ship. In a cabin below deck they saw a bed hung with silk, at the foot of which was a wonderful sword partly drawn from its scabbard. When the maiden saw that the sword lacked a belt, she left the room and returned moments later carrying a belt of extraordinary design.

'When I discovered this to be the ship that brought Joseph of Aramathea to Britain with the Holy Grail, I gladly cut off my hair so that the sword should not lack a belt,' said the maiden. She showed the knights the belt and on close inspection they could see that it was made of long, golden strands of hair woven with pearls and jewels and laced all together with gold threads.

As the ship sailed on unmanned, blown by a following wind on its uncharted journey, the maiden told the knights many tales connected with the vessel. After several days' they finally made landfall and the three knights saw that they had come to the shore of the wasteland kingdom of King Pelles.

The story now rests briefly with Sir Lancelot and what befell him on his quest to find the Holy Grail.

One day on his travels, realizing that night was rapidly closing and he had nowhere to stay, he saw a chapel in the distance and decided to rest there. However, as he approached the building he saw that it was entirely derelict: the roof had fallen in, broken masonry was scattered all around and weeds grew in the aisles. But as he looked up the nave he saw a most peculiar sight, for there was a fine altar, covered with a clean silken cloth upon which was set a golden, branched candlestick bearing six lighted candles. Some unseen barrier, however, seemed to prevent him entering the chapel, try as he might, and he could only marvel at the altar through the broken windows.

After his long, hard day of riding, Lancelot was very weary, so he lay down outside the ruined chapel and soon fell asleep. Some hours later, close to midnight, he was woken abruptly, and as he lay in that muddle-headed state halfway between sleep and wakefulness, he saw a strange sight: two damsels, each mounted on a palfrey, were riding up to the chapel, while behind them was a litter on which lay a sick knight.

'O blessed vessel, I beg you to heal me,' prayed the knight in great distress as his bearers carried him carefully into the chapel.

Lancelot was by now wide awake and through the windows he saw a wondrous sight, for there above the altar hovered the sacred vessel of the Holy Grail hidden beneath its veil of samite. The wounded knight struggled with all his remaining strength to rise from his litter and touch the sacred vessel, whereupon he was immediately healed.

At this sight Lancelot felt himself weighed down by the sins he had committed in his life. He longed profoundly that he could find a way inside this chapel and be healed by the power of the Holy Grail. As he remained deep in thought, a hermit came up beside him.

'Look your fill at this sight, Sir Lancelot, for it is all you are destined to see of the Holy Grail. The sinful thoughts you carry in your soul have rendered you unworthy to see the Holy Grail without its veil.'

'Is this a dream?' thought Lancelot as the hermit suddenly disappeared from sight and there was no other living person to be seen.

'Begone from this most holy place, unworthy knight,' spoke a mighty voice out of the star-bright heavens. And as the single word 'begone' echoed in his head, Lancelot began to weep piteously because he realized that he would never be worthy to look upon the Holy Grail or draw spiritual nourishment from its power.

He fell to the ground weeping, his arms outstretched as he clawed at the tinder-dry ground seeking somehow to ease his misery. Some time later he felt a hand rest gently on his shoulder as if to comfort him, and raising his mudstained face, he saw the hermit who had spoken to him earlier and who now regarded the stricken knight with a soft and gentle expression.

'Think, noble Lancelot, what little value there is in all your many gifts and deeds of chivalry if you hold wickedness in your heart that sins against the laws of both God and man,' said the hermit. His words touched Lancelot to the core of his being and he broke down afresh, confessing for the first time his adulterous love for Queen Guinevere. And so it was that Lancelot received absolution for his sinfulness and then continued on his quest to find the Grail, once more in a state of grace.

Guided as if by some unseen power, his adventures led him to the enchanted ship which had earlier transported the three knights to the waste-land kingdom. Likewise, when Lancelot stepped aboard this vessel it slipped

its moorings and sailed for many days, hugging to the shoreline where it anchored each evening. One night, tired of remaining on board, Lancelot made his way ashore. As he accustomed his swaying body to firm land, he heard a horseman riding towards him, and when the rider drew closer, he saw that it was the Red Knight with the white shield – his son Galahad. Both men walked towards each other, tears and smiles commingling at their reunion. Together they made their way on board the magic ship, which swiftly set sail again of its own volition.

Through many days they sailed on the open sea and each time they made landfall, they went ashore into unknown countries and followed many perilous adventures, battling with wild beasts and strange creatures they found in these territories. During this time father and son grew to love and respect each other more deeply.

When, once more, the ship lay at anchor off the very shore where Lancelot had first boarded, a richly-clad knight rode up leading a pure white horse by his right hand.

'Follow me, good Sir Galahad,' called out the knight, 'for now it is time to leave your father and return to the Grail Quest.'

Father and son embraced sadly because they knew in their hearts that this would be their last time together. After Galahad had ridden away, Lancelot returned to the ship where he prayed that he, like his son, might be found worthy to have sight of the Holy Grail. The very next evening Lancelot made his way ashore and, mysteriously finding his horse tethered near the shore, he rode inland until he came to a castle where two lions guarded the gates. The same portentous voice from the heavens instructed him to enter the castle if he wished to see what his heart desired. As he rode forward, a dwarf took his sword, for custom forbade that it be worn in this castle. Getting down from his horse, he heard the mighty voice call out to him once more.

'Enter within, Sir Lancelot, and you shall see what your heart desires.'

As he walked through the castle, the great doors swung open of their own accord, while all around him the air was filled with sweet and heavenly sounds. Walking further into the castle, he found himself inexplicably drawn to one chamber. He entered this place, which shone as bright as daylight with countless lighted candles, and he knew with certainty that the Holy Grail had been there. He fell to his knees filled with wonder and dread.

Suddenly, a mighty crack resounded through the air and a voice called out, 'Leave the chamber, unworthy Lancelot, or repent of this for the rest of time.' Although he knew he must move, he was rendered powerless to do so. An instant later, when the Holy Grail appeared, Lancelot was cast down on the floor in a dead faint and lay thus for twenty-four days and nights, as if dead. But at midday on the twenty-fifth day, Lancelot revived and found that his eyes were still dazzled with the marvels he had seen; it was as if he had been dead and seen paradise. However, he would not speak of these wonders which remained locked deep within his soul.

Close on a year and a day had passed since the start of the Grail Quest and Lancelot returned to Camelot where he told of his adventures and what had befallen his fellow questing knights to the eager court. From that time forward Lancelot wore a rough hair shirt next to his skin in penance for his adulterous love for Queen Guinevere. However, from the moment he saw her again he knew that he was powerless to cease loving this woman, who still remained the most important person in his life.

The story now returns to the three good knights who sailed in the magic ship until it reached the wasteland kingdom. Going ashore, they found their horses awaited them, so they immediately rode inland until they reached the devastated castle of King Pelles. As they rode through its ruined gates, the inhabitants came out in great excitement to greet them.

As soon as the knights entered the hall, they saw the frail figure of the maimed King Pelles, who was lying on a wooden bier so that the gaping wound in his side was clearly visible. He raised himself feebly to see who approached.

'Welcome, good knights, welcome,' he said, and wept to see his grandson Sir Galahad arrive in such splendour. 'The end of your quest is near, for tonight the Holy Grail will be in this castle.'

As night fell, an unearthly wind rushed through the castle. 'Let all unworthy men leave this chamber,' ordered King Pelles, whereupon everyone departed save the three knights and the king. As they waited expectantly, the room was filled with an overpowering heat, then the doors burst open to admit a procession of heavily veiled figures. As they glided across the hall, hardly seeming to touch the ground, the knights looked on in wonder. The first two figures carried tall, lighted white candles in heavy gold candlesticks. The figure following them held aloft a flat silver dish. Behind them was a figure, its head bent forward, carrying a spear. From the tip of this spear fell drops of blood, but the drops never touched the ground; instead, they vanished mysteriously. The final figure carried the vessel of the Holy Grail, which shone through its gleaming white veil.

The figures gracefully crossed the floor and each in turn placed the candlesticks, dish, spear and the vessel of the Grail on a silver table which had been positioned in preparation for this event. As the figures turned from the table to merge into the shadows, their angelic faces were momentarily visible. The knights knelt, filled with an overwhelming sense of peace and tranquillity.

The next moment a mighty voice boomed out: 'Draw near the Grail, Sir Galahad, for your whole life has been a preparation for this moment. You are without pride, greed, cowardice and all the weaknesses of men. Drink from this cup, Sir Galahad, earthly guardian of this most sacred relic. Guard it well so that only worthy men may look upon it in its full glory. In it they will glimpse the paradise that all men seek.'

Sir Galahad approached the table and with great reverence drew off the cloth. He lifted the vessel in both hands, raised it slowly to his lips and drank. As he returned the cup to the table, the assembled company knelt and praised God for the sights they had seen. At length Sir Galahad arose and looked towards his grandfather. Without a word he moved to where the king lay on his bier and placed his fingers on the wound in the king's side. Straight away, the gaping wound closed and was healed. King Pelles immediately rose to his feet and joyfully embraced Sir Galahad. Exactly as had been prophesized, the king's grandson had healed his wound and now his wasteland kingdom would be restored to life.

Once again the disembodied voice filled the hall: 'Galahad, make ready to leave this land. Tonight the Holy Grail shall pass from this kingdom, for the men in this land have grown wicked and it shall never be seen here again. Take Sir Perceval and Sir Bors with you as companions on your journey. The enchanted ship awaits where you left it. You shall escort the Holy Grail to the distant city of Sarras, which shall be its final resting place.'

The knights set out at once on their journey. From the torches which lit the castle's courtyard they could see that the kingdom of King Pelles had miraculously come to life again, for the air was filled with the sweet smell of roses that had suddenly bloomed in the warm night.

By daybreak the knights reached the enchanted ship and no sooner had they boarded the vessel, than it moved off from the shore. When they ventured below, they found the Holy Grail covered with a gleaming red cloth resting on the silver table they had seen at the castle.

For many weeks the ship sailed on its course at a gentle speed, as if conscious of its precious cargo. At length the knights sighted the city of Sarras and on making land the inhabitants came out to greet them. In this city the knights built a great temple to house the Grail, and when the king of the city died, the inhabitants begged Sir Galahad to be their king. Every day the knights went to pray before the Grail. Then, one day as they prayed, a voice

told Sir Galahad to draw nearer. As he approached it, a mighty beam of light descended upon him, shining with an unbearable intensity. When it passed the Grail was gone from its sacred resting place and Sir Galahad was no more to be seen. Both were taken up to heaven and the Holy Grail was lost to all men's sight for evermore.

Sir Bors and Sir Perceval grieved for the good knight who had been their teacher in all spiritual matters. They no longer wished to remain in the city of Sarras, so the two good men soon departed. Sir Perceval became a hermit and spent the remainder of his days in seclusion in distant lands; he died after only a year. Sir Bors, however, sailed once more for Arthur's kingdom where he related the glorious conclusion to the Quest of the Holy Grail.

The Decline of Camelot

Lancelot and Guinevere

WHEN THE GLORIOUS QUEST of the Holy Grail was concluded, a darkness fell over the kingdom of Britain, as the sacred relic with all its heavenly powers left the land forever. Many knights of the Round Table who had followed this quest failed to return to Camelot, for they had lost their lives in the adventure. In their stead new knights had taken their seats at the Round Table.

The long burden of ruling now began to take its toll on Arthur and he aged rapidly. It grieved him that Guinevere had never borne him children, so Mordred, his natural son by Morgan le Fay, was increasingly marked out as his heir. When Mordred had reached the appropriate age of knighthood, his

mother had sent him to Camelot, having discerned that with the passing years Arthur's rage at her malevolence had subsided.

Mordred had grown to be a wicked man, raised by his mother from infancy to do evil. At first the pale and fragile appearance of this youth caused people to be trusting of him rather than cautious. But as a glossy fruit may entirely conceal the putrefaction that seethes beneath its unblemished skin, so it was with Mordred. He began by sowing the seeds of resentment against his step-mother Guinevere. Then he wormed his way into the confidence of various dissatisfied knights, and before long he had gathered around him a loyal band of followers who talked treason against the king.

Although the blood in his veins ran thin through too close a kinship between his mother and father, Mordred's intelligence was sharp, and soon after arriving at court he had discerned the real depth of feeling that existed between Guinevere and Lancelot. He saw, too, that Arthur had blinded himself to their passion, being unable to accept, in kind with many others, that any such thing could exist between his beloved wife and his dearest friend.

Day by day Mordred grew increasingly impatient to wear the crown of Britain and was none too keen for nature to take its course. His mind was filled with bitterness against his natural father which had been nurtured ceaselessly by his mother.

Around this time Queen Guinevere organized a sumptuous feast in her private quarters for twenty-four favoured knights of the Round Table. To do these knights honour the queen had taken infinite care with the dishes that were to be served, ensuring that the menu included special delicacies especially favoured by each of her guests.

It was known throughout Camelot that Sir Gawain loved fruit, particularly apples, so the queen had ordered a bowl of perfectly ripened fruits to be placed near him at the table. However, before Sir Gawain had a chance to sample them, Sir Patrice helped himself to the choicest looking apple and ate it with obvious relish. Moments after swallowing the last bite, the hapless knight fell to the floor clutching his throat and choking for air. Finally, with a hideous rattling gasp, he died. The gathering immediately dissolved into uproar and all eyes were turned on the queen. She had prepared much of the feast with her own hands, so many knights began to hurl accusations.

'The queen has poisoned the fruit,' they shouted.

'She wished me dead,' shouted an angry Sir Gawain.

'She is guilty of murder,' said Sir Gaheris. 'She sought my brother's death.'

'The queen must stand trial,' said Mordred in a calm and quiet voice when the hubbub lessened. At these words the chamber fell silent as the seriousness of such an action was borne in on the knights. The feast broke up in disarray and soon the whole court was in turmoil at what had happened. Sir Gawain, one of King Arthur's most loyal knights, felt under threat, while the family of the poisoned Sir Patrice were crying out for vengeance.

Arthur now found himself in an intolerable situation. When he spoke to the queen, he knew beyond all doubt that she had not been responsible for the poisoned fruit. As a king, he knew there should be a trial, but as a husband he resisted such a course. Meanwhile, whipped up by Mordred's machinations, feelings at court ran high and would not subside of their own accord.

In addition, Mordred had circulated a wicked story that filled Arthur with foreboding when it reached his ears. Rumour had it that Guinevere and Lancelot had been driven so demented by their lust that they believed the only solution was to usurp Arthur's throne; it was also said that the queen had plotted to poison any possible heirs who might stand in their way, such as Sir Gawain who was nephew to the king. Lancelot, the rumour continued, had grown increasingly arrogant because of the glory his son Galahad had won in the Grail Quest, so he now believed himself worthy to be king.

Arthur wept when these rumours were related to him, for he saw them as the realization of Merlin's prophecy - that the destruction of the most glorious order of knighthood would be set in motion by the actions of his wife and his best friend.

Arthur's sorrowful duty as king impelled him to arrest the queen to face the charge of murder. After solemn counsel at the Round Table it was agreed that the queen's guilt or innocence should be determined by single combat: if the queen's champion overcame the champion selected by Sir Patrice's kin, she would be proved innocent.

As the appointed day for the joust drew nearer, still no champion had come forward to fight for the queen, which many people interpreted as a further sign of her guilt; not one person at court was ready to defend her honour, her life and her liberty. But where was Lancelot at this vital time? On his return from the Grail Quest he had vowed to leave Camelot rather than endure the continual temptation of seeing the queen, so he kept himself at Joyous Gard, where he distracted himself with countless knightly pursuits, hoping that he might one day feel able to return to court.

The day of the queen's trial by combat dawned but still no champion had been found to defend her reputation. It had been agreed that if, by the time the great church bell had finished tolling the eleventh hour no champion had come forward, the queen would be declared guilty of murder and burnt at the stake in punishment.

As the hour drew nearer, a deathly hush descended over the lists where those gathered pondered the increasing gravity of the queen's predicament. The king could scarcely contain his anxiety; his face was pale and drawn, while his hands grasped the arms of his seat so tightly that his knuckles appeared white. How could he have allowed such a situation to come about? The awful silence was broken only by the jangling harness of the grey horse to be ridden by Sir Mador, avenger of his cousin Patrice's murder.

'There is still time for the queen to find a champion,' thought Arthur with all the calm he could muster some thirty minutes before the eleventh hour. The queen sat rigid and ashen at her husband's side, as if carved of marble. Her lifeless features concealed the fear and torment that raged within her.

From where he sat, Mordred began to look increasingly satisfied, confident that the queen's fate was sealed. He was ready and eager to light the first bundle of twigs on the queen's pyre.

Suddenly, the faint but rhythmic footfall of a galloping horse could be heard riding frantically towards the gathering; in a short space the rider's outline could be seen. This sight breathed life and voice into the spectators, for surely this rider came to save the queen? With but a minute to spare the horseman galloped across the open ground that lay before the castle of Camelot. The knight was now clearly visible, dressed splendidly in white shining armour and wearing his visor down so that he could not be recognized. Nor could he be identified from his shield or lance, for he carried no device. Galloping still faster, the unknown knight raced towards the place of combat as the great bell in the church tower began to toll the eleventh hour.

'Surely this knight comes to defend the queen?' shouted Sir Bors above the murmurs of the crowd. 'If he is the queen's champion, we cannot pass judgement until he has been allowed to defend her.'

'No!' shouted Mordred emphatically. 'The queen has been proven guilty and so must die, for there is no one here to defend her.' He was determined that no last-minute champion would rescue the queen.

'Enough,' intervened Arthur. 'It is only just that this knight be allowed to fight for the queen if he comes in her cause.'

The sound of the bell died away as the knight finally reached the place of combat.

'Are you the queen's champion?' asked Sir Bors before any other person could speak. At this question the mysterious knight inclined his head and lowered his lance, thus silently establishing that he was here for that purpose.

Without delay the two knights fell into fast and furious combat, splintering many lances in the process. Eventually, the queen's valiant champion knocked Sir Mador from his horse and he fell to the ground, rendered senseless by his fall. This accomplished, the mysterious knight removed his helmet and the noble Sir Lancelot was revealed for all to see. At the sight of him the queen fainted away, and the king, who had looked so pale, began to breathe normally because he knew that his wife was saved.

Sir Lancelot was taken to the castle and his cuts were cleaned and soothed with healing balms. Within the week he was again anxious to leave the court, for he and Guinevere wished to give rise to no further gossip. But no one who witnessed the haunted expression in the couple's gaze, even when they were not together, could deny the thread that bound them. Nevertheless, as soon as he was able, Lancelot left Camelot for Joyous Gard.

Some time later, when court life had returned to normal, Arthur decided to clear his wife's name by calling on the Lady of the Lake to come to Camelot and disclose before the assembled knights of the Round Table who was guilty of Sir Patrice's murder. She revealed that one Sir Pinel had poisoned the fruit because Sir Gawain had slain one of his cousins. Arthur ordered that the true account of the poisoned apple should be engraved on Sir Patrice's tombstone, thereby exonerating the queen of all blame.

Mordred's evil stories, which had gained currency at court, now began to circulate throughout the land, undermining King Arthur's rule. After the near tragedy caused by the poisoned apple, an increasing number of knights became disaffected with the king for they believed his once strong rule had grown weak. It was but a short step for these disloyal knights to support Mordred.

Meanwhile, although the queen remained aloof from court matters, she continued to mistrust Mordred and knew that he wished her and Arthur dead. The king, however, would not listen to her words of warning on this matter.

Winter soon came round again and as the hours of daylight lessened, the darkness reflected the evil that slowly but surely took hold of Arthur's kingdom with a dreadful certainty. Malicious gossip repeatedly reached the ears of the king concerning Guinevere and Lancelot, yet he remained unflinchingly loyal to both these people whom he loved more than himself. By Christmas time Camelot was no longer the warm and joyful place it usually was and a cloud was cast over the festivities.

The cold and wearisome winter months dragged endlessly, then spring suddenly burst out, bringing warm and sunny days. Soon the land and everything growing in it began to bud and blossom vigorously as the earth renewed itself. This year the queen was determined to cast off the sorrows she had endured during the winter and welcome the spring with new optimism.

On May Day, a carefree festival when members of the court put aside their daily worries and fixed their minds solely on pleasure, Guinevere gathered around her a hand-picked band of knights and ladies and they began a merry jaunt into the forest to see what flowers and fruits the spring had brought in its train. They had risen early that morning and all eagerly anticipated the feasting and flirting that would ensue at the behest of the queen of the May, a role that this year fell to Guinevere.

As delicate and colourful as butterflies, the queen and some of her ladies were dressed in gowns as fine as gossamer garlanded with dewy blossoms, while their unbound hair was entwined with flimsy ropes of tiny flowers. The knights, too, were garbed traditionally, wearing the green attire of woodmen and, as custom demanded, carrying no arms.

Thus decked out as simple country folk, the merry band set off on their horses which were likewise festooned with floral garlands. A short distance into the verdant forest the revellers stopped in a clearing to dance and here they crowned Guinevere queen of the May with a garland of lady's mantle twined with trailing speedwell. The queen was full of joy, as she flirted with her chivalrous knights in the expected courtly fashion, and her ladies watched laughingly at their mistress's antics. Later they rode further into the forest, which echoed with their singing and laughing, while pages ran alongside blowing on trilling pipes and filling the forest with their excitement.

When the party grew hungry and thirsty, the pages ran ahead to find a place to set out the food that was carried in baskets on the horses' backs; fruits, white bread, meats and many delicacies were set upon white linen cloths, while golden jugs were filled with fruity wine. It was a scene in which the lusty god Bacchus would have been happy to participate. After they had eaten their fill the party grew silent as they rested in the warm afternoon sunshine that dappled the ground in the forest clearing. It was well into the afternoon before

195

the revellers revived and made ready to return to Camelot.

Unknown to the queen, one of the knights present – Sir Meliagraunce – had loved her from afar for many a year. Now, filled with wine and made bold by the heady spring day, his infatuation and lust for the queen knew no bounds. How simple it would be to make the queen love him as she was known to love Sir Lancelot, he thought. Fortunately, for this presumptuous knight, Sir Lancelot, who would have killed him for daring to have such thoughts, was far from Camelot at his castle, Joyous Gard.

As the lighthearted troop of revellers made their way back through the forest, Sir Meliagraunce stormed up to the queen, crashing through the trees and taking her roughly from her horse. At first Guinevere and her ladies mistook his motive, thinking it was all part of the day's amusement, so they played along with this clumsy knight's desires and acted their parts with much jollity. The queen laughed gaily, feigning indignation at being an abducted maiden, but then something in Meliagraunce's expression suddenly made her mirth turn to anxiety. As he rode deeper and deeper into the forest with her, and far away from her companions, she began to feel greatly frightened.

Sir Meliagraunce's abduction of the queen was by no means spontaneous. He had, in fact, made countless preparations for this moment, rebuilding and heavily fortifying a tower that belonged to him in this very forest. As he rode to this destination, the queen frantically wondered how she might escape.

When it became clear to the ladies that the queen had genuinely been abducted, they trotted in pursuit as fast as they could on their timid palfreys, but they could not keep pace with Meliagraunce's powerful stallion.

'Come back, come back!' shrieked the ladies repeatedly, hoping that their cries would reach the knights who had ridden ahead of them to Camelot on their faster horses. 'Come back, the queen is taken!'

When the knights eventually heard their distressed cries and realized that something was amiss, they rode back and learned what had happened.

'A curse that we are unarmed!' exclaimed Sir Gawain. 'This treacherous knight has surely planned all this because he knew we would be unarmed today. I swear to kill this wretched man the moment I catch up with him.'

However, more important than vengeance was to rescue the queen. Discounting the fact that they were unarmed, the fearless knights galloped off along the forest track, hastily following the path of Meliagraunce's horse. As they rode, they saw to their mounting horror that items of the queen's apparel were strewn along the way. Guinevere was obviously in great danger.

Meanwhile, as they could not assist in the pursuit of the queen's abductor, the ladies made their way back to Camelot with all the speed they could muster. When they reached the castle, they rode straight into the great hall, calling all the while for someone to save the queen.

That day it so happened that Lancelot was passing by Camelot on a pilgrimage to a holy shrine; when he heard the dreadful news, he rushed at once to offer King Arthur his services.

'I must rescue the queen. I cannot rest until she is safe and Meliagraunce is dead,' said Sir Lancelot, his voice quivering with emotion.

'So be it,' replied Arthur, knowing that now the queen would be swiftly saved from danger. Embracing Lancelot, he called for his finest horse to be saddled and bade him mount it. The king then wished Lancelot Godspeed and watched his departing figure charging across the green landscape towards the forest, afire with his mission to save the queen.

Once Meliagraunce had reached his tower the queen was unceremoniously locked in a chamber which had been magnificently furnished: heavy silk rugs hungs on the walls and covered the floors; a bed was draped with curtains of the finest silk the East could supply; the air was perfumed with the heady richness of an exotic oil; and on a delicately carved table stood a golden flask of fine wine. An old mute serving woman, who had never known any world beyond this castle, was sent to wait upon the queen. She served Meliagraunce with unswerving loyalty and therefore would not help the fair stranger to escape, however much the woman pleaded.

In addition to this loyal serving woman, Meliagraunce's watchful retainers were standing guard at all points of exit and skilled archers were placed as lookouts on the topmost battlements.

Before long the first knights of the queen's party had reached the tower and, although they were unarmed, they rode up fearlessly with every intention of storming the tower. However, as the unarmed men drew close, they were shot down by the archer's cruel arrows and ten noble knights were badly wounded in their honourable defence of their queen.

Meliagraunce had, of course, anticipated that an attack would be launched against him, so he had hidden thirty of his finest archers in the branches of the trees near the castle and ordered them to shoot down any knight who ventured there. As Sir Lancelot stormed out of the forest, he was met by a rain of arrows; miraculously he escaped unscathed but his unfortunate horse was killed beneath him. This incident only increased his rage because without a horse he could not reach the castle. Then, through the trees, he saw a cart approaching which was drawn by two broken-winded nags. Stopping the driver, he discovered that he was delivering barrels of water to the tower.

'I will give you fifty pieces of gold if you take me into the tower,' said Lancelot.

Now this was riches beyond the poor man's wildest dreams, so he readily agreed to Lancelot's request. On reaching the tower, the barrels, including the one in which Lancelot was hidden, were hoisted into the fortification. No sooner was the consignment safely delivered than Lancelot burst out of his barrel, scattering its wooden slats and metal hoops all around him.

'Where is the queen?' cried Lancelot. 'Where is the traitor Meliagraunce?'

The terrified servants seemed to have lost the power of speech, so without waiting for an answer Lancelot rushed to an open doorway and up a spiral staircase that led to all the rooms. Scouring every chamber and slaying any person who stood in his way, he soon found the captive Guinevere. She blanched and then blushed as she saw that Lancelot had come to save her.

Walking quickly over to the queen, Lancelot took her in his arms and held her close. When their lips met, a flame of desire was ignited that would never be extinguished. Guinevere felt she never wanted to move from Lancelot's arms, and he too longed to hold her forever. Suddenly, Meliagraunce appeared in the doorway, sword in hand, for he had heard that an interloper had penetrated the defences. When he saw Guinevere and Lancelot embracing, his jealous rage broke loose. Lancelot instantly drew his sword and turned to face Meliagraunce, ready to fight.

'You will die for what you have done. There shall be no mercy for you,' warned Lancelot, his voice as cold as the hard steel of his blade.

'We shall see,' retorted Meliagraunce defiantly, although his voice betrayed his apprehension. The two men were within striking distance of each other, but just as they were about to cross swords, the queen cried out.

'Have not enough good men died today?' asked the queen. 'I do not wish to see another drop of blood spilt.' Crossing over to where the two men stood, her hand touched Lancelot gently on his fighting arm.

'Meliagraunce did me no harm. He has treated me most courteously. Put up your sword and make your peace with him,' said the queen. Lancelot, who could deny the queen nothing, did as he was bid, for he could not kill a man whose only crime was to desire the queen. Now, instead of killing the nervous Meliagraunce with a swift sword thrust, Lancelot extended his right hand in a gesture of peace.

Sir Meliagraunce was greatly relieved with this change of humour and began to treat Guinevere and Lancelot as if they were honoured guests. But all knew in their hearts that this was mere pretence and that trust was not entirely restored. In addition, Meliagraunce was the only man to witness the love-

making between Lancelot and Guinevere, and who knew what mischief he might make with this knowledge? However, that night they all ate in the dining hall, as courtesy demanded, and much food and wine were consumed. At last Sir Meliagraunce made as if ready to retire for the night.

'It has been an adventurous day,' he said, 'and I feel much fatigued.'

'Yes, I am also ready to retire,' said Guinevere, and as she spoke these words her gaze was drawn to Lancelot who was staring at her intently.

Sir Meliagraunce was not about to allow these lovers to bill and coo unobserved, for he knew if he were to witness their lovemaking it could do him great good with Sir Mordred and his supporters. Thus, he went to the room adjoining the queen's bedchamber where there was a peep-hole cut in the wooden partition and waited to see if the lovers would lie together that night.

It was not long before Guinevere and Lancelot retired to their respective chambers to make ready for bed. The tower rapidly fell silent as all its inhabitants lay down to sleep, but there were three people who got no sleep that night. A little after retiring, when Lancelot judged he would be unobserved, he climbed silently down the stone staircase to the floor below where Guinevere slept. Without knocking, he opened her unbolted door and went over to the luxuriantly draped bed. Sweeping back the curtains, he found Guinevere awake and waiting for him. There was no need for words as all through the night the lovers who had been separated for so long loved each other.

From his spyhole Sir Meliagraunce clearly witnessed the goings-on in the queen's chamber and his jealousy would not allow him to sleep. He vowed not to rest until he had killed Sir Lancelot, even if it cost him his own life.

Next morning Sir Meliagraunce was not surprised to discover that his guests, who only yesterday would have given up their lives in an attempt to leave the confines of his tower, today showed no inclination to depart. For all his civility, Meliagraunce seethed with silent but deadly anger and was made entirely treacherous by his jealousy.

'I have always admired your deeds of chivalry,' said Sir Meliagraunce after Lancelot had broken his fast. 'It would give me great pleasure while you are my guest if you would accept a gift which I believe is worthy of your knighthood.'

'I will gladly accept your gift,' said Lancelot, who was in such good humour that he looked on Meliagraunce as his gentle host instead of his vile captor.

'Then come with me,' said Meliagraunce. The two men made their way down the stone stairway to the cellars. 'We have no mews in this tower, so I keep my favourite falcon in the cellar. It suits the bird very well, for he prefers darkness and is startled by any sudden light.'

Lancelot's thoughts were all on the queen who rested in the chamber above, so Meliagraunce's invitation to the cellar to see the bird caused him no anxiety. He certainly had no premonition of what happened next. No sooner had Lancelot walked a couple of paces into the cellar than Meliagraunce pushed him to the ground, slammed the door shut with a mighty crash and locked him in. Lancelot was now Meliagraunce's prisoner and he cursed himself for being so easily duped. His troubled thoughts were now of how he could defend the queen if he was himself a captive. He felt wretched and full of foreboding at what Meliagraunce might have in store for the defenceless Guinevere.

However, Meliagraunce did not intend to make mischief in the way Lancelot feared. He confined the queen in her chamber and left her closely guarded while he rode off to Camelot, intending to meet secretly with Sir Mordred and tell him what had passed the previous night.

For two days Lancelot languished in the cellar and with each passing day he grew more afraid at what might have befallen the queen. His anger grew, too, because he was quite powerless to escape. Then, on the third day, a maiden came and unlocked the door, for she was exceedingly curious to see the great Sir Lancelot with her own eyes.

'Give me three kisses and I will help you to escape,' said the maiden, pursing her full red lips together provocatively.

This seemed a small price to pay, thought Lancelot, so he did as the maiden asked. However, she was bitterly disappointed with this good knight's kisses for he merely pecked both her cheeks and kissed her hand with such lack of feeling that she burst into tears. His kisses showed that all his passion was saved for the queen alone. Nevertheless, the little maid kept her part of the bargain: she led Lancelot out of the tower and fetched him a horse to ride, and he immediately set off for Camelot.

Speed informed all his actions, for he wished to find Sir Meliagraunce swiftly and then hasten back to free the queen who was still held captive. However, as fate would have it, Lancelot's path through the forest led him right into Meliagraunce, who blanched at his misfortune to run into the enraged knight. Lancelot showed the traitor no mercy and lopped his head right off. But sad to say, this deed was done too late, for Meliagraunce had already imparted his damaging news to Mordred and his followers.

Without delaying, Lancelot returned to the tower to liberate the queen, conducting her back to Camelot where there was universal rejoicing that she had been rescued from her terrifying ordeal. For the first time in a long while Arthur felt his land was at peace because all immediate dangers, that until recently had lapped at his heels like floodwater, had unexpectedly subsided.

However, the men who desired his destruction merely bided their time until they judged they could usurp King Arthur of Britain's throne.

After his love for the queen had been consummated, Lancelot could not bear to be away from her, so to her great joy he returned to Camelot, filling his days with all manner of knightly activity. He took part in many combats and vanquished many churlish and wayward knights, bringing honour once more to the somewhat tarnished reputation of the knights of the Round Table. However, these endless feats merely served to distract him from the wearisome times when he could not be with the queen.

A year passed quickly by and Mordred continually watched Lancelot to see if he could surprise him with the queen, but they

were so discreet in their assignations that he was entirely unsuccessful. Finally, he grew so frustrated that he and his cousin Sir Agravaine, his closest confidant and brother to Sir Gawain, decided to take matters into their own hands. They went to King Arthur and told him all they knew about the goings-on between the queen and Sir Lancelot. The king, of course, refused to believe anything they said, but eventually he could not disregard their words. In fact, a certain distance now existed between the king and the queen. He no longer visited her bedchamber as a husband should, and when they were together she was always distracted, as if preoccupied with other matters. The intimate confidante who had been his close companion through so many years seemed to have left him.

Arthur would never have believed it of himself, but in recent times he had begun to take heed of the rumours that circulated at court. Finally, he agreed that if Mordred found proof of Guinevere's adultery, then he should bring it to him. This was, of course, all the incentive that Sir Mordred and Sir Agravaine had been waiting for.

A short time later Mordred suggested that King Arthur let it be known one day, especially to his attendants, that he was going hunting and would be away from the castle all night. In fact, he would return at midnight with Mordred and his followers hoping to surprise the lovers in the queen's quarters. That night all went according to plan and thus they surprised Lancelot in the queen's bed.

Although cornered like a wild beast in a trap, Lancelot fought to save the queen and himself, killing or maiming anyone who tried to take him prisoner. Eventually, with superhuman strength, he managed to escape from this ambush and fled from the castle, taking to the forests where his loyal cousins Sir Bors and Sir Lionel rode out to meet him. Here, he judged, he would be better able to rescue the queen if he were a free man. Other knights also rode out to meet him, for they chose to ally themselves to his cause rather than endure the machinations of Mordred who was mistrusted by all true men. Soon a growing band of knights followed Lancelot to Joyous Gard where he took refuge from this present disaster.

Meanwhile, the queen was accused of high treason and sent for trial. This time there was no doubt that she would be found guilty; and the penalty for her crime would be death by burning at the stake. The trial took place in the great hall at Camelot, the scene of so many joyful occasions in the past. Seated in serried ranks, the court looked on gravely as the queen, frail and worn since her captivity, swayed slightly as she stood to hear of what she was accused. There were many knights and ladies who were heavy of heart and kept their eyes downcast, not daring to meet the gaze of the queen. No one doubted her guilt but some thought she need not die so cruelly. All could see that the king was greatly exercised at what lay before the queen. Only Mordred and his supporters were of good cheer as they revelled in the thought that each day brought closer the time when Mordred would be king. Perhaps, fittingly, Mordred had been named chief prosecutor at the trial and in this role he unleashed all the pent-up rage he harboured against the king and queen.

Before long, all the bishops and knights of the Round Table, sitting in judgement, passed sentence on the queen. She was found guilty of high treason and within three days was to be burnt at the stake. At these words the queen swooned and had to be helped away from the hall by her handmaidens. All she could hope was that King Arthur would grant her clemency so she would not suffer a hideous death in the flames.

Arthur, however, knew that he was powerless to change the penalty the law set down, whatever his private longings might be. To interfere would undermine all that he had struggled to achieve throughout his reign - justice for all people, whatever their rank or offence. None the less, he did not wish Guinevere to suffer the agony of death by burning, so later that day he handed one of her waiting ladies a strong sleeping draught that he instructed was to be given to the queen before she was led to execution. This quick-acting drug would sedate the queen and ensure that she would be unconscious before the flames even licked around her body.

Word of Guinevere's fate swiftly reached Lancelot and his loyal band of knights. Indeed, Lancelot too had been condemned to death in his absence; if he were captured, he would be stripped of his knighthood, taken to a place of execution in a cart and hanged - an ignominious end for a former knight.

Two days before the date set for the queen's execution, Lancelot and his supporters rode from Joyous Gard intent on rescuing Guinevere. They rode ceaselessly through the night and the following day, for they knew they could not tarry if they were to be in time to save the queen.

Recent events had irreparably divided the loyalties of the knights of the Round Table. The noble fellowship seemed reduced from its former glory to worthless ashes. During the last dreadful days Arthur had lost strength and vigour and was now a listless and aged man. Merlin's prophecies seemed about to come true.

Arthur dared not allow himself to visit the queen because he knew that if he did he would surely pardon her. Sir Gawain begged most passionately that the queen's life might be spared but to no avail. Indeed, Arthur was surprised that he should intercede for Guinevere because Agravaine, his brother, had been killed by Lancelot when Mordred and his followers had surprised the lovers in the queen's bedchamber.

It was to have been Sir Gawain's solemn duty as the premier knight of the Round Table to escort the queen to her execution, but he refused to undertake this distasteful task, requesting that his brothers Gareth and Gaheris should do this sorrowful duty in his stead.

All were agreed that Lancelot would attempt to save the queen and it was to be the responsibility of the two Orkney brothers to prevent her being rescued. This troubled Gareth and Gaheris because in defending the queen they might well endanger Sir Lancelot whom both loved well. Gareth, especially, wished him no harm, for he had been dubbed a knight by Sir Lancelot.

To add to their worries, if the queen were rescued, civil war seemed certain to follow. This, however, was exactly what Mordred wanted, so he could usurp the throne. His mother, Morgan le Fay, had now ventured to court for the first time in many long years, for she was determined to ensure that nothing untoward should happen to her precious son. As a gift for him, she brought a wonderfully fashioned suit of armour that was imbued with her strongest magic; when her son wore it in battle he could not be slain.

The morning of the queen's execution dawned. There were many tears shed in the castle that morning and even warrior knights were seen to blink away tears that filled their eyes. Gareth and Gaheris, dressed in monks robes and their heads bowed heavy in sorrow, made their way to the queen's chamber. Guinevere was dressed in a light shift with her hair hanging loose; in her hand she held a bag of gold to pay the fee to her executioner. Her face was pale and drawn, and she felt glad that her parents had not lived to see this day. She had removed the seal ring that Arthur had given her on their wedding day which marked her out as queen of Britain. Now her thoughts were consumed with Lancelot and in the last remaining hours she had realized that she really preferred to die if she could not be with him. As she walked to the door one of her handmaidens came forward with the king's draught in a golden goblet.

'Drink this wine, my lady. It will warm you,' she said.

'I shall soon be warm enough,' replied the queen, but seeing the distress in her faithful companion's eyes she drank deeply. Immediately, she felt strangely relaxed, as if floating.

'Take some more, my lady,' urged her maid, and the queen did so.

Gareth and Gaheris did not reveal their identity to the queen. In silence they led her along the chill corridors lit only by the spluttering light of reed torches. They descended the vast stone stairway that led through to the great hall. Here they crossed to the door that opened into the courtyard and once outside the queen saw the bundles of twigs and straw that were piled high around the wooden stake.

Straight as a reed, the queen walked over to the pyre. The executioner came forward with silken ropes with which to bind her to the stake. As custom demanded, he begged her forgiveness for what he did, which the queen gladly gave him. Then she pressed the bag of gold into his hand so he would perform his task with all possible speed and humanity.

Suddenly, Queen Guinevere's limbs seemed to melt beneath her and she could barely stand upright or keep her eyes open. Thinking that she seemed faint, the executioner hastened to make everything ready.

Nothing would impel Arthur to attend the execution. He remained in an upper room which overlooked the courtyard unable to believe that Lancelot had not yet come to rescue the queen. In fact, there had been no sight or intelligence of Sir Lancelot's whereabouts, so the guards had relaxed their stance. Just as a torch was put to the pyre, pandemonium broke out in the courtyard – a trap door was lifted and out of the ground rose Sir Lancelot fully armed and closely followed by ten fearsome knights. Lancelot had discovered the plan of the subterranean passages beneath the castle from Sir Gareth, who had become familiar with them from his time as a kitchen boy.

A great thumping was heard at the gates of the castle and the next instant another of Sir Lancelot's supporters rode in leading a string of eleven fine horses. The knights all rushed to their mounts, then, with their swords drawn, they held back the guards so that Lancelot could cut Guinevere free and carry

her off to safety. Fortunately, the fire had not yet taken hold, so with one slash of his mighty sword Joyous, Sir Lancelot freed the queen, lifted her on to his horse and galloped out of the castle, quickly followed by his band of knights.

From where he watched high above the courtyard, Arthur could breathe once more, for the two people he loved best in all the world were now gone and free from immediate danger. However, in the preliminary skirmish, the unarmed Gareth and Gaheris, who had been nearest to the queen, had been struck down and killed by Lancelot himself. Their grief-stricken brother Gawain had not been roused to vengeance when his brother Agravaine had been killed by Lancelot, but now he was driven into a frenzied rage at these futile deaths. Two great knights who had brought much honour to the glorious brotherhood of the Round Table were needlessly dead.

Rushing to Arthur, Gawain demanded that an army be raised and sent to destroy Lancelot and his supporters for this heinous deed. Thus, Gawain in his grief unwittingly allied himself to Mordred's cause, for the good knight had sworn that he would not rest until Lancelot's own blood was spilt in retribution for his brothers' deaths.

The fugitives rode at speed from Camelot for several days, never pausing, only pressing forward to increase the distance between King Arthur's forces and themselves. At last, they reached Joyous Gard, galloped in behind its walls and closed the gates fast to make ready for the siege that would surely follow.

Meanwhile, at Camelot Sir Gawain toiled day and night as if demented to see that an avenging force was quickly raised and equipped. In but a short time, the army was ready to depart and make an assault on Lancelot's castle, which they planned to raze to the ground and slay all those who dwelt within its walls.

Throughout the days of frantic preparation, Gawain's fevered mind turned over and over how Lancelot must be destroyed for the deaths of his noble brothers. His thoughts often returned to his childhood years that were spent on the westernmost island of Orkney where he and his brothers had roamed freely like wild creatures, learning their skill with weapons which brought them fame in later life. He remembered how they had taken a special delight in keeping each other amused in the family's cold, dark castle with fabulous stories of the glory each would win when made a knight. Now, not one of his brave brothers would gain further glory - only a cold grave in the inglorious earth. When he thought of their exuberant vitality so wantonly extinguished, the pain of their deaths caught and twisted his heart afresh.

The avenging army marched to Joyous Gard. With Arthur at its head, it descended from Camelot and rode through the land until close to Joyous Gard where Lancelot awaited the attack. For several months, under the rigorous command of Gawain, the avenging army lay siege to the castle. Eventually Lancelot sent a messenger to Gawain saying that his knights would rather fight a pitched battle than remain under siege for perhaps many more months. So it was agreed that battle should commence within two days.

On the appointed day, there was fierce and prolonged warfare, and it distressed many that the knights of the Round Table should be fighting each other. At the end of the day, Lancelot called for a truce, saying that he preferred to return the queen to her husband as long as he was given an assurance that she would not be harmed. He also promised to go into exile across the sea to his father's castle at Benwick. Through his emissary, he begged Arthur to agree to these conditions before any further knights were slain. To show his goodwill Lancelot immediately made his farewells with Guinevere, each knowing that this might be the last time they would be together. Then the queen rode away from Joyous Gard and crossed the field of battle to return to her husband.

This gentle offer of peace may well have appeased Arthur, but Gawain still burned with rage that Lancelot lived. He argued that he should not be allowed to escape with impunity and urged that an army should be sent to Benwick to destroy him once and for all. The majority of the king's knights were in agreement with Gawain, so Arthur reluctantly agreed that they should once more wage war on Lancelot. As Arthur was to lead this expedition to France with Gawain at his side, he left Mordred as the regent of his kingdom. Now nothing could impede his evil offspring from seizing the throne.

Aided and abetted by his mother, Morgan le Fay, Mordred immediately began to plunder the royal treasury. Now that his power was absolute, he soon began to indulge in all manner of depravities, placing no check upon his cruel appetites. However, in order to deceive his father, he sent daily missives that all went well in Britain, so Arthur was untroubled about his kingdom.

Meanwhile, in France King Arthur's army lay waste to Lancelot's land, burning his fields and fouling his wells, while that good knight remained within the strongly fortified and well-provisioned Benwick Castle. Lancelot heartily wished to end this futile war, so he sent a damsel bearing an offer of peace, but more than once this offer was unceremoniously rejected.

Daily during the siege Sir Gawain would stand beneath the castle walls and throw down a challenge to the besieged knights. A few of Lancelot's followers, who could not contain their anger at his insults, would venture out to fight him, but Gawain would strike down whichever man rose to his challenge.

Although he was slaying Lancelot's knights daily, it did not lessen his grief and anger – it was Lancelot alone that he sought to kill. At last, however, Sir Lancelot could no longer tolerate Gawain's taunts, so he came out to fight him in single combat.

It so happened that an enchanter had put a spell on Sir Gawain so that he was possessed of three times his normal strength for the three hours before noon each day. When Lancelot came out to fight at ten o'clock in the morning, he was hard pressed to stay alive, so overpowering was Gawain's strength. But barely had noon passed when Gawain suddenly grew listless and Lancelot was able to wound him.

Gawain lay sick for three weeks but as soon as he could ride his horse again, he stationed himself below the walls of Benwick Castle.

'Come out you coward,' he cried. 'Come out you traitorous knight. Come out Lancelot and fight me once more if you dare.'

Eventually, Sir Lancelot could bear the taunts no longer, so he put on his armour, mounted his fine charger and rode out of the castle to meet Sir Gawain. Once more they fell into ferocious combat and Gawain's morning-time strength came close to destroying the mighty Lancelot. Then, as before, Gawain faded on the stroke of noon and Lancelot struck him such a ferocious blow on his barely healed wound that Gawain fell to the ground writhing in agony. This time, it was a month before Gawain's wound was healed again.

Events might have continued thus for many wearisome months had not ominous news arrived from Britain that Mordred had seized the throne and crowned himself king. Later reports said that Mordred intended to wed Queen Guinevere but that she had hastily taken refuge in the great tower in London which was now under siege by Mordred.

Sick at heart, Arthur immediately raised the siege of Benwick Castle and returned with all possible speed across the sea to Britain, fearful at what further sorrows might await him on his return to his beleaguered kingdom.

When Arthur arrived at Dover, Mordred was waiting to do battle with him. The forces of father and son met at Barham Down outside the ancient town of Canterbury and a hideous battle was engaged. Many good and loyal knights were slain, as brother fought brother and cousin fought cousin in this wretched slaughter. At the end of the day's fighting, when Arthur rode around the battlefield carnage to see who had died, he came across his well-loved nephew Gawain lying half dead from his wounds. Without delay he was carried to the king's tent where his injuries were dressed. Knowing that his end was close, Gawain called for writing materials and with the little strength remaining to him, he wrote a letter to Lancelot.

To Sir Lancelot, the very flower of knighthood, Sir Gawain, son of King Lot and nephew of noble King Arthur salutes you.

One day past I was struck again in that same wound you gave me before Benwick Castle and now I am near to death. I sought this wound and blame you not for it, fair Lancelot. But I beg you for the love we once shared that after my death you will come once more to Britain, and pray at my grave for my eternal soul.

I beseech you and your noble knights to come with all haste so you may rescue our great king, for he is in great peril of losing his crown and life at the hands of his traitorous son Mordred. When we landed in Dover on the tenth day of May, he was there to fight us with his rude army. That time we put him to flight but he will soon return with an increased force. It was in this same battle that I was mortally wounded.

Mordred has declared himself king of this sorry land and would take Queen Guinevere as his wife had she not sought sanctuary in the cathedral in London.

I am close to my death now and I beg you as my life ends you will return to Britain with all Godspeed.

Sir Gawain signed the letter, marked it with his seal and two hours later was dead. He was buried that same day in Dover Castle, close to where he died. This brave knight's final wish that his letter might find its way swiftly to Lancelot was the last service rendered to him by King Arthur.

When, some time later, Lancelot received Gawain's letter, he was angry to discover Mordred's treachery. Without delaying he and his followers made ready to return to Britain, hoping that they would be in time to help Arthur rout the evil Mordred's army.

The Last Battle

KING ARTHUR LED HIS ARMY WESTWARD through the country until he reached the plain of Camlann where it had been agreed that on the day following, Trinity Sunday, the final battle should take place.

On the night before battle, Arthur was plagued with a terrible dream in which he saw himself sitting on a cloth of gold while deep beneath him in hellishly black water writhed serpents, worms and many other horrible beasts.

The king screamed in horror and woke in a cold sweat. Later, when he lay down again on his bed, he thought he saw Sir Gawain ride through the quiet camp on his best loved horse.

'Gawain!' cried Arthur to his sister's son. Then it seemed that Sir Gawain entered the king's tent followed by countless ladies for whom he had fought as champion; throughout his life Gawain had always been known as the knight who fought for women.

'Do not fight tomorrow, Uncle,' said Gawain's ghost. 'These good women's prayers have brought my spirit to your tent tonight to warn you of your certain death if you fight tomorrow. Sue for peace, I beg you, if you wish to live. Keep at peace for a month and a day and then your kingdom will be saved, for in that time Sir Lancelot and his loyal knights will have come into this land to fight with you. Lancelot is the knight to free the land of Mordred's evil.' Having spoken, Gawain's ghost vanished.

The king rose at once from his bed and called a counsel of his wisest men to tell them of his dream. They all heeded what Arthur related to them and as the first chilly light brightened the sky, four of King Arthur's most valued counsellors rode over the plain of Camlann to Mordred's camp to sue for peace as Gawain's ghost had advised.

As they rode across the open heathland, they saw at close quarters the appalling strength of the enemy: more than 100,000 warriors, armed and fully equipped, their powerful horses champing at the bit, were ready for battle to begin. That morning the four wise men won a fragile truce for Arthur but neither side stepped down from their readiness to do battle. Each leader instructed his warriors that if even one sword were drawn by the enemy, then the war trumpets should sound and battle would commence. Fourteen chosen knights from each side, who were to be exchanged as guarantees of each side's good faith, rode forward to the opposing ranks. Meanwhile, Arthur and Mordred rode to the middle ground. A squire then rode up to them bearing a golden cup filled with wine and each man in turn drank from it to set a seal upon their truce.

No sooner had both men drunk, than an adder slid from beneath the gorse bushes on the heathland where the armies were pitched. This slender serpent slithered along the ground without a sound until it began to curl itself around the chainmail-encased leg of one of Mordred's knights. When this man looked down and saw the serpent entwined there, he drew his sword and let it fall on the venomous creature.

Like a beacon flaring on a pitch dark night, this knight's burnished blade caught the sunlight and its glinting steel signalled the end of the truce. The cry

of battle resounded around the plain and the two forces bustled with activity as men made ready to do combat.

'Oh, unhappy day that knights should fight in mortal combat against their brothers-in-arms,' said Arthur, as he led his army into the field.

Never in the whole history of the kingdom had there been a more doleful battle. Horses reared at each other as if marking the beginning of some great tournament, but as the warriors pitted their strength against each other and the air resounded with the clash of steel on steel and the screams of those who were

hurt, there was no doubt as to the ferocity of the fighting. Many knights lost their mounts and were to be seen ducking, weaving and thrusting at their adversaries from the ground; soon many fine knights had fallen dead to the hard, cold earth.

All through the battle, King Arthur rode with inexhaustible energy and foolhardy bravery, riding straight into the ranks of Mordred's forces and relentlessly seeking out his fiendish son so he might destroy him. Both armies fought viciously throughout the day, and as the light faded, a mist came rolling in from the sea and shrouded the battleground like a burial sheet, masking the horrific carnage for a short time. A deadly hush fell over the plain and Arthur struggled to see which of his good and loyal knights remained alive at the end of the day. With a numbed heart he discovered that only two knights remained alive - Sir Bedivere and Sir Lucan - but both were wounded.

'Are all my brave knights gone?' murmured Arthur in disbelief, for the very flowers of knighthood were now lying bloody and lifeless on the heathland. Despite terrible weariness, he would not withdraw or rest until he discovered whether Mordred had been killed. Slowly he made his way through the carnage, stopping sometimes with tears running down his cheeks as he came upon the corpse of some knight dear to him. Seeing a body propped up, he thought for a moment he had found another of his knights alive. Then, as the mist lifted, he spied his reviled son leaning breathless and bloodied against a ghastly pile of corpses.

'Bedivere, give me a spear for I will kill my son. I shall not besmirch Excalibur with his evil blood,' said Arthur, as he drew closer to where Mordred stood.

'Sire, leave the battlefield. Do not linger, I beg you. Remember Sir Gawain's warning,' urged Sir Lucan. 'Spare your son, at least spare him until this day is done, otherwise I fear for your life.'

'I may never again have such a chance to rid the world of his evil,' said Arthur as he rushed forward, lance held in readiness, at his accursed son. 'Turn and fight if you dare for I will kill you.' Arthur's voice floated over the plain where it was heard by Mordred who stopped quite motionless. Then he turned to look at his father and bent down to clean his sword's bloodied blade on a dead man's cloak. He did not shrink from this engagement, for he believed himself to be invincible through the magic suit of armour his mother had given him. Advancing towards his father, he lifted his visor so that Arthur could see the hatred in his eyes.

'Die, you devil's spawn,' cursed King Arthur, raising his spear above his head to strike. Father and son were now upon each other. Without hesitating,

Arthur let loose the spear, which flew straight and true towards Mordred's throat. Suddenly, all the witchcraft that surrounded Mordred dissolved and the spear pierced his neck as if it were made of gossamer. Mordred let out a gurgling groan and fell forward as his life blood gushed from his body and a ghostly pallor came over him. Whimpering faintly as the blood pumped from his fatal wound, Mordred fell to the ground dying.

'You should have died as soon as you were born,' said Arthur, filled with a bitter sadness. His anger was all spent as he bent down to end the agony of his dying son. Thinking that Mordred was muttering to him, Arthur bent down to listen. Rallying the last of his strength, Mordred lifted his sword which had

fallen by his side and thrust it deep into Arthur's body. This done, Mordred then died. Arthur immediately removed the sword from where his son had plunged it, but knew he was fatally wounded.

'Carry me above the battlefield where I may breathe some clear air,' whispered Arthur to Sir Lucan and Sir Bedivere who had rushed to aid him. The two knights did as requested, but they knew the king had not long to live. On a mossy hill overlooking the plain, as the fiery sun dipped lower and lower in the west, they laid Arthur on the soft turf, leaning his head gently against the trunk of a tree. However, this effort proved too great for the wounded Sir Lucan and he died soon afterwards. Sir Bedivere alone remained to guard the king and as he knelt by him the brave knight wept.

'Do not grieve for me,' said Arthur. 'I will soon be gone to a place where my wounds will be healed.' This only caused Bedivere to weep afresh. Then Arthur told him there was one final service he could perform for him.

'Take Excalibur to the land of lakes that lies over the brow of yonder hill and throw it into the first lake you come to. You will know it by the straight rushes ringed about it. Return and tell me what you see,' said Arthur.

Bedivere rode off but when he stood by the water's edge he could not bring himself to do as he was bid. Instead, he hid the sword in the rushes and rode back to where Arthur lay.

'What did you see?' asked Arthur.

'Nothing but the waves ruffling and closing over the sword as it fell beneath the water,' said Bedivere.

'You lie,' said Arthur. 'Return again and do as I ask you.'

Once more Bedivere returned to the lake. Taking the sword from where he had hidden it, he looked upon its wondrous beauty and again he could not cast it into the lake where it would be lost for all time. He hid it again and returned to where Arthur lay sinking fast.

'What say you now?' asked Arthur.

'It was dark, Sire, and all I could hear was the lapping of the waves,' replied Bedivere.

'Are you a traitor, too?' demanded Arthur. 'You have betrayed me twice. Do you deceive me so that when I am dead the sword may be yours? By delaying you put my life in jeopardy.'

For a third time Bedivere rode to the lake but this time he walked out into the water as far as he could and, holding the sword by the tip of its blade, he hurled it with all his might out over the lake. It rose and circled high into the air, twirling as it fell down to the water. And as it fell, a woman's hand swathed in gleaming white samite rose from the lake and caught hold of the sword by its hilt. The arm shone brightly, creating its own light, and she brandished the sword three times in the air before sinking once more below the waters. Bedivere hastened back to where Arthur lay and told him of the marvellous sight he had seen.

'Alas,' said Arthur. 'I have tarried too long here. Good Bedivere, carry me down to the barge that awaits on the river that runs nearby.'

At the water's edge a barge was moored on which stood three queens dressed in black mourning robes with chaplets of gold set around their brows. The barge, too, was swathed in black mourning drapes. When the queens saw that it was Arthur who was brought to them, they wept to see the great king so injured.

'Place me in the barge, Bedivere,' said Arthur faintly, and the knight did so gently, as the three queens moved forward to receive him. One of these queens

was his sister Morgan le Fay, her anger now all spent and the wickedness that had dominated her life all gone. There, too, was Arthur's other sister, the queen of Norgales, together with the queen of the wasteland kingdom. Finally, the beauteous Lady of the Lake, guardian of the Vale of Avalon to which they would bring the king, came forward.

'Oh, my dearest brother,' cried Morgan le Fay with great emotion as King Arthur's head rested on her lap. 'What has been done to you? You are quite chilled, for you have tarried in this place too long. We must hasten away.'

As Arthur looked up into Morgan's eyes he saw in them a new-found gentleness and peace, the hatred that had once filled them now resolved.

Trailing its mourning drapes in the still water, the barge moved off on its own accord to where the river flowed into the great lake where Arthur had first gained the mighty Excalibur. The barge floated across the waters of the lake until a chain of small islands that could just be discerned in the distance. When the floating bier reached this place, the boat moved out of men's sight, disappearing into the mists that almost obscured these islands. They had at last journeyed into the magical Vale of Avalon where Arthur would be healed of his wounds. No mortal man can venture into this magic place for it is that realm where heaven joins the world of man. It is in this magic kingdom that Arthur lies waiting to this day, whenever his country should need him.

Bedivere wept at the king's leaving. He alone witnessed the passing of King Arthur, high king of all Britain and founder of the most noble order of chivalry, the Knights of the Round Table, whose glory shall live in men's minds until the end of time.